LOUIS XIV AND THE
AFFAIR OF THE POISONS

Borgo Press Books Edited & Translated by FRANK J. MORLOCK

Anna Karenina: A Play in Five Acts, by Edmond Guiraud, from Leo Tolstoy
Anthony: A Play in Five Acts, by Alexandre Dumas, Père
The Children of Captain Grant: A Play in Five Acts, by Jules Verne and Adolphe d'Ennery
Crime and Punishment: A Play in Three Acts, by Frank J. Morlock, from Fyodor Dostoyevsky
Don Quixote: A Play in Three Acts, by Victorien Sardou, from Miguel de Cervantes
The Dream of a Summer Night: A Fantasy Play in Three Acts, by Paul Meurice
Falstaff: A Play in Four Acts, by William Shakespeare, John Dennis, William Kendrick, and Frank J. Morlock
The Idiot: A Play in Three Acts, by Frank J. Morlock, from Fyodor Dostoyevsky
Jesus of Nazareth: A Play in Three Acts, by Paul Demasy
The Jew of Venice: A Play in Five Acts, by Ferdinand Dugué
Joan of Arc: A Play in Five Acts, by Charles Desnoyer
The Lily of the Valley: A Play in Five Acts, by Théodore Barrière and Arthur de Beauplan, from Honoré de Balzac
Lord Byron in Venice: A Play in Three Acts, by Jacques Ancelot
Louis XIV and the Affair of the Poisons: A Play in Five Acts, by Victorien Sardou
The Man Who Saw the Devil: A Play in Two Acts, by Gaston Leroux
Mathias Sandorf: A Play in Three Acts, by Jules Verne and William Busnach
Michael Strogoff: A Play in Five Acts, by Jules Verne and Adolphe d'Ennery
Les Misérables: A Play in Two Acts, by Victor Hugo, Paul Meurice, and Charles Victor Hugo
The Mysteries of Paris: A Play in Five Acts, by Eugène Sue and Prosper Dinaux
Ninety-Three: A Play in Four Acts, by Victor Hugo and Paul Meurice
Notes from the Underground: A Play in Two Acts, by Frank J. Morlock, from Fyodor Dostoyevsky
Outrageous Women: Lady MacBeth and Other French Plays, edited by Frank J. Morlock
Peau de Chagrin: A Play in Five Acts, by Louis Judicis, from Honoré de Balzac
A Raw Youth: A Play in Five Acts, by Frank J. Morlock, from Fyodor Dostoyevsky
Richard Darlington: A Play in Three Acts, by Alexandre Dumas, Père
The San Felice: A Play in Five Acts, by Maurice Drack, from Alexander Dumas, Père
Saul and David: A Play in Five Acts, by Voltaire
Shylock, the Merchant of Venice: A Play in Three Acts, by Alfred de Vigny
Socrates: A Play in Three Acts, by Voltaire
The Stendhal Hamlet Scenarios and Other Shakespearean Shorts from the French, edited by Frank J. Morlock
A Summer Night's Dream: A Play in Three Acts, by Joseph-Bernard Rosier and Adolphe de Leuwen
Urbain Grandier and the Devils of Loudon: A Play in Four Acts, by Alexandre Dumas, Père
The Voyage Through the Impossible: A Play in Three Acts, by Jules Verne and Adolphe d'Ennery
The Whites and the Blues: A Play in Five Acts, by Alexandre Dumas, Père
William Shakespeare: A Play in Six Acts, by Ferdinand Dugué

LOUIS XIV AND THE AFFAIR OF THE POISONS

A Play in Five Acts

by

Victorien Sardou

Adapted and Translated by Frank J. Morlock

The Borgo Press

An Imprint of Wildside Press LLC

MMX

Copyright © 2010 by Frank J. Morlock

All rights reserved. No part of this book may be reproduced without the expressed written consent of the author. Professionals are warned that this material, being fully protected under the copyright laws of the United States of America, and all other countries of the Berne and Universal Copyright Convention, is subject to a royalty. All rights, including all forms of performance now existing or later invented, but not limited to professional, amateur, recording, motion picture, recitation, public reading, radio, television broadcasting, DVD, and Role Playing Games, and all rights of translation into foreign languages, are expressly reserved. Particular emphasis is placed on the question of readings, and all uses of these plays by educational institutions, permission for which must be secured in advance from the author's publisher, Wildside Press, 9710 Traville Gateway Dr. #234, Rockville, MD 20850 (phone 301-762-1305).

www.wildsidebooks.com

FIRST WILDSIDE EDITION

CONTENTS

Cast of Characters 7

Act I, Scene 1: Escape 9
Act I, Scene 2: Chatelet 22
Act II: The Fortune Teller 47
Act III: The Grotto of Thetis 100
Act IV: La Reynie's Office 140
Act V: The King's Palace at St. Germain 178

About the Author 206

DEDICATION

To

JACKIE STANTON, AKA DAGNY, FOR HELPING ME WITH THIS AND NUMEROUS OTHER PLAYS.

CAST OF CHARACTERS

L'Abbé Griffard
King Louis XIV
Colbert
La Reynie
Louvois
Carloni
Hector de Tralage
Desgrez
de Brionne
de Dommeyrac
Lulli
D'Aquin
Sagot
De Cessac
Lesage
De Visé
D'Estrées
L'Abbé Guibourg
An usher
A peasant

Madame de Montespan
La Voisin
Mademoiselle D'Ormoize
Mademoiselle Desoeillets
Madame d'Humières
Madame de Nevers
Madame de Brissac
Marguerite, Voisin's daughter
Margot
Madame de Feuardent
Madame Lamperier
Madame de Jeancourt
Madame de Vitry

ACT I

Scene 1

Escape

A hill on the right bank of the Var, near the village of La Gaude. In the background the Var is clearly visible, and around it the countryside of Nice. In the distance, the heights of the Alps. Towards the right, the sea, the Bay of Anges. Nice and its old Chateaux. Olive trees, rocks at right. Everything is brightly lit by the sun.

(Griffard and Carloni enter. They are dressed wretchedly. Pants formerly red are almost black with dirt. Rough shirts, naked feet. On his head, Carloni has a ruined straw hat, deformed. Griffard, a torn handkerchief. Carloni climbs the trunk of a tree and looks through the branches to the left.)

Griffard
You see them?

Carloni
No. They have given up pursuing us.

Griffard (looking around)
Where are we?

Carloni
Near La Gaude.

Griffard
That village down there?

Carloni (coming down)
Yes. Since these peasant dogs learned that galley slaves have escaped, they are like madmen, to hunt them, to be the first to catch them.

Griffard
Small wonder they have recognized us for galley slaves with these scarecrow's clothes we are wearing to replace our prisoner's clothes.

Carloni
They have a flair for it. Here we are sheltered and can breathe a little.

Griffard
Yes. Since yesterday evening, we have run like— Fortunately, you know the country.

Carloni
Yes, I am from Nice, which you can see from here. See the old Chateaux?

Griffard (looking)
Then, that's the Var River?

Carloni
Once on the other side, in the territory of the Duke of Savoy, we will have nothing more to fear! You don't know anyone?

Griffard
No one! But I have a sister in Holland to whom I will write to get money.

(Griffard sits, but never ceases to be on the alert, uneasy.)

Carloni
And we will burn candles to St. Laurent, my patron, for the ill but lucky wind which dashed our galley on the rocks of Moines and permitted us to escape. Our comrades would have done better to come with us. This is the shortest way and the most certain.

Griffard
Yes, but we must cross the Var.

Carloni
As soon as night falls—but the water is deep. You see those little black islets? We have to swim from one to the

other. You know how to swim?

Griffard
Very well!

Carloni
Me, no! But you will help me! I was lucky to escape with you.

(Carloni sits on a big stone before the tree.)

Carloni
Were you a long while in the galleys?

Griffard
For more than two years.

Carloni
Me, three! What did you do for that?

Griffard
Nothing. Politics.

Carloni
You are a priest?

Griffard
No.

Carloni
They call you "The Abbé."

Griffard
Abbé, yes, but not priest like the Italian Monseigneur. Abbé of the court, professor of philosophy and belle letters history, later Greek and, moreover, gazetteer.

Carloni
And for this, they put you in chains?

Griffard
For opinions not in agreement with those of Mr. Louvois.

(Carloni is still uneasy, he gets up and goes to look to the left while still talking.)

Carloni
Good! There must be something you're not saying.

Griffard
There is nothing else.

Carloni
Well, as for me, they got me for having killed a man with a knife in Marseilles for cheating me at dice. And the funny part is that when they arrested me under the name of Carloni, they didn't know they were looking for me under the name of La Fleur for a much worse affair. The death of the Duke of Savoy—you must have heard tell of that—you who read the gazettes.

Griffard
Yes. That was four years ago. The Duke died suddenly—

poisoned they said.

Carloni
That's right! The one who did it was named Chasteuil. (coming back to sit on the stone) Ah, there was a fellow who had some adventures. Imagine, he was a Knight of Malta and Captain of the Guards of Monsieur the Prince de Condé! Then suddenly, without anyone knowing why, he became a pirate. He was captured by the Barbary pirates and sold as a slave in Algiers. When he ransomed himself, he came to Marseilles, where he took religious orders and then he became prior of the Carmelites. He introduced a young girl into his convent. She became pregnant—that embarrassed him—he strangled her and buried her in the church.

Griffard
Oh!

Carloni
They caught him and were going to hang him. At the foot of the gallows he was delivered by his friend the Captain de Vanens and some soldiers! They both went to the Duke of Savoy who made Chasteuil the captain of his Guards of the White Cross and tutor of his children. It was then I met him and then that Chasteuil, with the help of Vanens, de Cadejan, a Paris banker, de Bachimont and two others—familiar friends of the Duchess, poisoned the Duke during a hunt.

Griffard
And you managed that?

Carloni
With them, and very well paid! Two thousand ducats, which I will find in Paris where I hid them with a lady of one of my friends.

(Carloni starts to rise.)

Griffard (holding him)
And the others—your accomplices?

Carloni
Oh, the others—not a chance. Cadejan, Bachimont, and Vanens—denounced. By whom? No one knows. All in prison. And Chasteuil died at Verceil, unfortunately, for we were planning something even better than that. Damn! How thirsty I am!

Griffard
Perhaps you will drink more than you want, crossing the Var.

Carloni
In one hour! Too long! I think I heard something over there. (pointing to the right) A noise of running water. I've got to see if there's a spring.

(Carloni walks past Griffard.)

Griffard (holding him)
If you are seen!

Carloni
Bah! They're a long way off.

(Carloni leaves with caution.)

Griffard
He's an abominable rogue. And if I did what I would like, I'd burn him alive for politeness. But still! A comrade in misery! Who has shown me a good road and who will drown if he crosses the Var without my help— I can't do that. But, on the other side, when we are safe! Triple rogue, with what joy I'll bury you there.

(Carloni returns. As he does so, he is shot from the left. He screams and falls. His straw hat rolls in the dust.)

Carloni
Bandit! He killed me.

(Griffard runs and pulls him up to a sitting position.)

Griffard
An unfortunate man.

Carloni
Ah! My holy patron saint! I am dead!

Griffard (opening Carloni's shirt)
I don't see any wound.

Carloni
Yes! Yes! In the side. It burns. Ah, God! God! I suffer. Oh!

(Carloni faints.)

Griffard
Yes, yes, here. I see it. Come, courage, courage.

(Griffard tears his shirt to stop the blood.)

Carloni
Oh! Poor, poor me! I cannot run or swim again.

Griffard
Yes, yes! I will carry you.

Carloni
Oh!

Griffard
Shut up! I hear them! Shut up!

(Griffard stifles Carloni's cries with his hands. Three peasants pass to the left with old hunting muskets. They don't see the fugitives.)

First Peasant
I tell you, there are two.

Second Peasant
One alone, I tell you, with a straw hat.

Third Peasant (finding the straw hat)
Who does this belong to?

Second Peasant
For sure, I have touched him.

Third Peasant
He escaped that way—towards the Var. Take the bloodhound. I'll go this way.

(The three peasants exit.)

Griffard (to Carloni)
They are gone.

Carloni
Ah! Me, too, I'm going—I feel death freezing me.

Griffard
Oh, no.

Carloni
Yes, yes! In a state of mortal sin—without confession. A sinner like me—help me—I am choking, and burning. Can you confess me? Give me absolution. Quickly, hurry!

Griffard
But, I cannot do it! I am not a priest, I told you that.

Carloni
Oh, wretched thing I am. I will be damned. I am going to hell—I don't want to! I don't want to! Ah! Holy Madonna. Pray for me, poor sinner! I repent. Don't damn me!

Griffard
No! No!

Carloni (breathing hard)
Ah! Listen, to save my soul, listen.

Griffard
Yes!

Carloni (gasping for breath)
You will go! Oh, God, give me the strength, I am choking. You will go to Rue Beauregard at Paris, near the Church of Bonne Nouvelle—

Griffard
Yes.

Carloni
Find the home of La Voisin—she's a well known palm reader—the friend of de Vanens, Chasteuil and several of the others! My mistress! It's with her I hid my ducats in the garden, behind a bench. My treasure. (raging) Ah! Holy Christ, to die without profiting from it. (trying to

rise, then falling back) No, no. Forgive me, my sweet Savior, pardon! I repent of it. I repent! Then, you will split it with her and have masses held for my soul. You understand clearly?

Griffard
Yes.

Carloni (in a weakened voice)
For two years—the time to get me out of hell. And don't cheat! Unless you do that, I'll haunt you. Masses every day! Every day!

Griffard
Yes! Yes!

Carloni
I can't see any more. Oh, poor, poor Carloni. It's all over for you. And without confession. Damned, you are damned.

(Carloni dies. The voices of the peasants returning can be heard.)

Griffard
It's over! They're almost here. Goodbye, poor devil.

(Griffard slips out. The peasants come back.)

Third Peasant
Where can he be, our little pigeon?

Second Peasant
He must have fallen nearby. (seeing the body) There you are, old boy.

(They run to the body. One kneels, listens to Carloni's heart, and raises his arm, which he then lets fall.)

First Peasant
Dead.

Second Peasant
Stone dead.

(They uncover their heads. Then they put down their muskets and get ready to carry the body.)

Third Peasant
And the other one?

Second Peasant
Ah, there was no other one!

CURTAIN

ACT I

SCENE 2

Chatelet

At Chatelet, the office of La Reynie. A large window in the rear. Chimney on the right front. Arm chairs. At left a small sofa. Little table at back. To the right of the sofa a chair. Entry door at back and a door to Sagot's office.

(La Reynie is seated in an armchair to the right of the table. Desgrez is standing in front of the table.)

La Reynie
You have the reports from the evening guards?

Desgrez (reports in his hands)
Yes, monsieur. Two murders. One in the Rue de la Calandre. The guilty party has been arrested. (he places a paper on the table) The other on the Pont Neuf Bridge. An unknown was thrown in the river by two guards of the King and a musketeer who have taken flight. (places another

paper on the table) Finally a woman, raped by lackeys who have taken refuge in the Hotel de Soissons, a place of asylum.

La Reynie
This is a flagrant abuse, these places of asylum, Desgrez.

Desgrez
On the subject of abuse, Monsieur Lieutenant General, the woman Gilberte, to be arrested at the behest of her husband for notorious misconduct, was seen yesterday in the Rue St. Antoine. She took refuge in the Church of St. Gervaise, where she was lost in the crowd, thanks to her mask. (placing another report before La Reynie, who files them in a file drawer) The mask is constantly playing us these tricks.

La Reynie
Yes, it's a detestable thing, this tolerance of women going masked in the street and in church. I intend to speak to the King about it. Go on.

Desgrez (reading another report)
The vandals persist in extinguishing lights that the Lieutenant General has placed in the streets.

(Desgrez places the report before La Reynie, who puts it with the others.)

La Reynie
Naturally. At Versailles, which isn't lighted, the nocturnal

outrages are more frequent than at Paris. Is that all, Desgrez?

Desgrez
Yes, monsieur.

(Desgrez withdraws to the window, ceding place to Sagot who takes his place at the table.)

La Reynie
And you, Sagot?

Sagot (two papers in hand)
A letter from the Grand Confessor of Notre Dame, who warns us of a fact worthy of attention. The Confessors of Paris declare that for some time they have been alarmed by the number of women who accuse themselves in confession of having given philters, powders or other drugs to their husbands before sickness or death carried them off.

La Reynie
That fact has already been brought to our attention.

Sagot (after placing the letter on the table)
And something even more grave—they send us, from the Church of St. Paul, this writing found in the confessional. (puts a tiny letter before La Reynie) It denounces a plan for poisoning His Majesty (La Reynie and Desgrez start) by the friends of Monsieur Fouquet who despair of obtaining his pardon while the King lives.

La Reynie (reading the letter)
Without other indications?

Sagot
None.

La Reynie
Here's work for you, Desgrez.

Desgrez (placing the letter in another dossier)
One hears tell, monsieur, of sudden, inexplicable deaths! This is worse than the time of La Brinvilliers.

Usher (entering and announcing)
Monsieur the Chevalier de Tralage.

La Reynie (interrupting him and rising)
My nephew? Let him enter!

(The usher goes to the door and makes a sign to Hector, who enters while Sagot and Desgrez go out. The usher disappears, closing the door.)

Hector
Sir!

La Reynie (calling)
Don't go far off, Desgrez. (to Hector) At Chatelet, Hector, at this time of day? You are early. Are you coming from Saint Germain?

Hector
No, monsieur! I slept at Paris and thought I'd profit by paying you my respects.

La Reynie
You come just on time. I need to speak to you. But first, what was this quarrel, day before yesterday, while playing with the Queen?

Hector
Nothing serious. We were playing at quatre with the Marquis de Civry who was cheating. I said to him: "But monsieur, you are cheating." He replied to me: "It's possible, monsieur, but I don't like to be told so." Bold as brass. I simply got up, bowed, turned my back, and he continued to play with the other two.

La Reynie
Who permit cheating?

Hector (gaily)
Oh, monsieur! If one took care about things like that, no one would ever play again. Everybody cheats, even at the King's table—under the pretext of outwitting cheaters. It would all pass quietly if Monsieur de Grammont didn't boast of it.

La Reynie
And the consequences of this affair?

Hector
None.

La Reynie
Forget that then, and let's talk about more serious matters. Take a seat. I have to reprimand you.

(Hector sits in the chair. La Reynie on the couch.)

Hector
Me, monsieur?

La Reynie
Yes, I brought you from Auvergne to place you as the secretary of Madame de Maintenon, whom you were lucky enough to please. And just when you were on the way to honors and fortune, you have stupidly appeared as an admirer—of whom? Of the favorite of the day, Mademoiselle de Fontanges. To compete with the King! Have you lost your mind?

Hector
Oh, monsieur. Calm down a bit. It is true I was taken with Mademoiselle de Fontanges, who has not discouraged my passion.

La Reynie
True, Monsieur Fool.

Hector
But I am only on the outer fortifications, I assure you.

La Reynie
By God! Mademoiselle de Fontanges is young, vaporish, coquettish. It pleases her to be courted by you. But she is not a woman to sacrifice the King for you. Still, it is already talked about that people take seriously the attentions you pay her.

Hector
Permit me, monsieur, to tell you, monsieur, how this gallantry came into being.

La Reynie
I know it. You knew, at the home of Madame de Soubise, a young girl, her servant Mademoiselle D'Ormoize, who you courted with success. Mademoiselle D'Ormoize, having left the service of the Princess for that of Mademoiselle de Fontanges, as Lady of Honor, you naturally frequented the salon of her new mistress, whose charms seduced you to the point of desolating the poor D'Ormoize, over whom you triumphed by promising her marriage.

Hector
Do you make it a crime for me, monsieur, to have seduced a Lady of Honor? The King has given us enough examples.

La Reynie
The King is the King—and doesn't promise marriage. It is the promise which is blamable.

Hector
Oh, sir, women find a pretext to justify their defeat.

La Reynie
If I am well informed, Mademoiselle D'Ormoize hasn't done that and she passed for a very honest girl before you knew her.

Hector
True enough, monsieur, but she is only a provincial, a little bourgeoise with neither relatives, nor fortune, and who has nothing except a fine education, lively intelligence, beauty, wit and tenderness.

La Reynie
Oh, but—

Hector
Oh, monsieur, you are not going to force me to marry her?

La Reynie
No, since she had the weakness to go with you, dispensing with that condition. But what I exact from you is that you terminate your attentions to Mademoiselle de Fontanges. They will surely awaken suspicions of a police more vigilant than mine—that of women who are jealous of her. Let Madame de Maintenon hear of it and you will be in great shape. You will get your dismissal and ruin all our hopes. Understand that of the three women disputing for the heart of the King, Madame de Maintenon is the one who will get him! Madame de Montespan is already passé. The

King is tired of her pride, her demands, her rages, her mad prodigality for gambling.

Hector
Yesterday, again, at the Queen's table—a loss of seven thousand crowns.

La Reynie
The present favorite, Mademoiselle de Fontanges, is very precarious. Her health is deplorable. The King doesn't like sick-abed ladies, witness La Vallière. The favor of your idol will wither with her charms, which are waning already. Madame de Maintenon is very healthy, of a robust beauty that defies ages. She's a wise, careful and easygoing person. Look at the road she took from the day she became a widow and governess of the King's children. And she did it without crossing any court ladies, of whom she recently said to me: "Their ignorance, their coarseness, their laziness, their eating, their tobacco, their liquors—all this is opposed to my taste and my reason, such that I cannot stand them." She has taught the King a tender, discreet affection, whose charm is great, had she given him nothing more. You are well placed to know it.

Hector
That's so, monsieur. His Majesty comes almost every day to talk with her, in the afternoon between three and four, without mystery, and nobody accuses them of a more complete intimacy.

La Reynie (rising)
She is the future, I tell you! Mademoiselle de Fontanges will be eclipsed, then the struggle will be between Venus/Montespan and Pallas/Maintenon. And Pallas will carry the day because the King's age demands wisdom.

Hector
I think so, monsieur.

La Reynie
Then, attach your fortune to hers, my dear child. Be on guard against this bad atmosphere of the court which she detests. Don't imitate those young libertines who parade their vices, nor those who mask it under a false devotion. Be wise and circumspect and your future is assured.

Hector
Here's what I'll do, monsieur. From tomorrow, I will break off all commerce with Mademoiselle de Fontanges.

La Reynie
About time! As for Mademoiselle D'Ormoize—

Hector
You will be content with me, monsieur—marriage apart.

La Reynie
Ah! Madame de Maintenon won't look on that with so bad an eye. She will recognize Mademoiselle d'Aubigne in this young girl! We will talk about it again. Are you going back to Saint Germain?

Hector
Only this evening, monsieur. I dine with the Duke of Vendome, with the Duchess de Bouillon and Madame de Tingry, who is going to take us to a fortune teller.

La Reynie
What childishness.

Hector
They are bored. Will I see you tomorrow evening at Versailles where there's to be a concert in the grotto?

(The usher enters.)

La Reynie
Assuredly. Till tomorrow, Hector.

(Hector bows and leaves.)

La Reynie (to the usher)
What is it?

Usher
A stranger who solicits the honor to be received by Monsieur the Lieutenant General.

La Reynie
His name?

Usher
Griffard.

La Reynie
Let him speak to Monsieur Sagot.

Usher
He insists on speaking to you alone, monsieur, having, he says, to reveal facts of the greatest importance.

La Reynie
How does this person appear to you?

Usher
Very well, monsieur, with an open face.

La Reynie (standing before the sofa)
All right. Let him come in.

(The usher goes out, signaling to Griffard to enter, then closes the door behind Griffard.)

Griffard (bowing)
I thank the Lieutenant General for the honor—

La Reynie
Let's make it quick. I am in a hurry. You have, you said, some revelations to make to me.

Griffard
Some very interesting ones.

La Reynie
Pardon! (sitting on the chair) But, first, to whom have I the

honor to speak?

Griffard
The honor is mine, monsieur. The Abbé Griffard, professor of belle letters and philosophy! My name ought not to be unknown to you.

La Reynie
Griffard? Yes, a vague idea!

Griffard
I am an Abbé without the priesthood.

La Reynie
I see. An Abbé of the Court.

Griffard
My father was a rich draper and destined me for the Church. But I had no vocation, none at all. At the death of my father, I split the inheritance with my sister, married to a merchant from Amsterdam, and I led such a joyous life that in five years I had spent it all on gambling and women. It was then I came to the Prince de Conti and became tutor of his sons. He had me take the collar in the hope of a benefice. Unfortunately, His Highness had fallen into such exaggerated piousness that, after having protected Moliere, he wouldn't allow me to applaud his work.

La Reynie (impatiently)
Pardon me, but these revelations—

Griffard
I am coming to it, monsieur. I'm getting there. On the 26th of June, 1678, I went out, and when I returned I found my lodgings invaded by the police. Monsieur Desgrez was in charge. I was taken here and interrogated by a drunken and enraged person, who put under my nose a manuscript of mine commenting on some court and town menus. I was not about to deny I had written this work, and the next day I was sent to Toulon at the express order of Monsieur Louvois and consigned to the galleys for five years.

La Reynie (startled)
The galleys?

Griffard (tranquilly)
I left.

La Reynie
Pardoned?

Griffard
Escaped.

La Reynie
You escaped?

Griffard
You would, too—from such a hell.

La Reynie (rising)
It is my duty to send you back.

Griffard
Without listening to me?

La Reynie (ringing)
Let's find out more precisely who you are! (to the usher who appears in the doorway) Tell Monsieur Sagot to bring me the dossier of The Abbé Griffard.

Griffard (to the usher) Honoré Griffard.

(The usher goes into Sagot's office.)

La Reynie
And how did you escape?

Griffard
Sheer luck! The galley broke up on the rocks near des Moines.

(Sagot returns with the dossier.)

La Reynie
Ah, here's the dossier. (reads it) Honoré Griffard, gazetteer! For libels, five years in the galleys.

Griffard
For libels! May I ask who denounced me to the police as an author of libels?

La Reynie (returning the dossier to Sagot)
You hear, Sagot?

Sagot
You yourself, monsieur.

Griffard
Me?

Sagot
By this letter. (handing him a letter) Which you ought to recognize.

Griffard (looking at it)
Ah, yes. I wrote it to my sister, but I left it unfinished and never mailed it.

Sagot (putting the letter back in the dossier)
Well, the post isn't for everything! The case is very interesting. The Abbé wrote without doubt before his window?

Griffard
Yes, on a little table.

Sagot
And the Abbé left?

Griffard
Yes.

Sagot
Without carefully closing the door and the window—so that an air current blew it into the street.

Griffard
Into the street!

Sagot
Where it was picked up by a passerby who took it to the Commissioner of the Quarter.

Griffard
The beast!

Sagot
And an immediate investigation resulted in the discovery of this manuscript. And letters dated from Amsterdam which made people think you were in correspondence with the Gazetteers of Holland, hostile to His Majesty.

Griffard
Never in my life!

La Reynie (reading the letter)
They must have believed it! Give a seat to the Abbé, Sagot, and retire.

(Sagot brings up a chair and leaves.)

La Reynie
Very rigorous, I admit. The galleys for five years.

Griffard
Say in perpetuity, monsieur. When one is in one of those, one never leaves.

La Reynie (closing the dossier)
Let's let that pass, Monsieur Griffard. We will try to forget it, if you have not come to tell me fairy tales.

Griffard
I think I would be stupid to come here with fairy tales—to throw myself in the lion's den.

La Reynie
That is why I am ready to listen.

Griffard
I don't care to be an informant, but my conscience told me that if I let these murderers work in peace, I was making myself their accomplice.

La Reynie
But, what murderers are you speaking of? Get to the point! The point!

Griffard (discretely pulling his chair towards La Reynie's armchair)
Sir, you have surely never forgotten the words of La Brinvilliers when put to the question: "If I am killed, I will be made to die for others!" nor her scream on the scaffold: "I am suffering for others—for others!" These words must have rung in your ears every time one spoke of poisoning—rightly or wrongly—at the death of Madame, of the Court of Soissons, of Monsieur de Lionne and most recently, rightly this time, at the time of the sudden end of the Duke of Savoy.

La Reynie
Rightly? What makes you think that?

Griffard
The confession of my comrade in escape, Carloni, who was implicated in this affair, the Chevalier de Chasteuil, the one who poured the poison died at Verceil. You held three of the accomplices, Monsieur de Bachimont, the Chevalier de Vanens, and the banker Cadejan, whose trial you managed in the background, for fear of too vividly lighting the face of she who ordered everything. The widow!

La Reynie (excitedly)
Much lower! You know all this too?

Griffard
You see!

La Reynie (leaning toward Griffard)
Continue, monsieur, continue.

Griffard (coming still closer to La Reynie)
Sir, am I not advising you of the existence of a secret society of malefactors—French, English and German—who from London, to Brussels, to Paris and Turin have their agents, their spies, their bankers, their factories, their depots of injurious instruments, their meeting places where they plan their fruitful operations, be it for their profit, be it on orders? From time to time you capture, by chance, one of their henchmen, but the band escapes you. I am of-

fering you possibly the means to throw over this gang a vast net. It will be all profit for Monsieur Colbert if, in exchange for a galley slave, I give him a certainty of the highest quality.

La Reynie
How's that?

Griffard
I think I've discovered the headquarters of the conspiracy, one of the most active factories and the most frequented shops.

La Reynie (quickly)
Which is?

Griffard
Easy, monsieur. Of this haunt, I have the vaguest indications, and I am only relying on the somewhat confused advisories of a dying man. Let's not scare the game. I am in a way to learn more through trickery than you through violence, by ingratiating myself into a world that I am eager to see close up to complete my studies of the morals of my times. In twenty-four hours I will know what I have hold of. I will be able to say to you: "Here's the cellar where they do their killing." You will then take over. The rest will be your business and that of Monsieur Desgrez.

La Reynie (standing)
Whose aid you will need, right?

Griffard (effacing himself to let La Reynie stand)
Assuredly.

La Reynie (ringing)
He is there! You don't suspect, Monsieur Griffard, the importance of the service you are rendering us. (the usher appears) Call Desgrez. (the usher leaves) Have you learned nothing concerning the King?

Griffard
Nothing.

La Reynie
Well, I am warned that his life is threatened by the friends of Monsieur Fouquet. Read this.

(La Reynie gives the letter to Griffard.)

Griffard (reading)
The life of the King! Ah, but no! His big dauphin of a son would much regret it.

(Griffard places the letter on the table. Desgrez enters.)

La Reynie
Enter, enter, Desgrez. (pointing to Griffard) An old acquaintance.

Desgrez (bowing)
I had the pleasure of arresting the gentleman once—Rue St. Louis-en- L'Île.

Griffard
And courteously. I recall it.

La Reynie
Monsieur Griffard possesses precious intelligence on the malefactors of whom we were speaking before his arrival.

Desgrez (graciously)
Oh, monsieur is one of them?

Griffard (quickly)
Not at all! What an idea!

Desgrez
Then, monsieur is one of ours?

Griffard
But, not at all!

Desgrez
Pardon, I thought—

La Reynie
Desgrez, you will follow to the letter the instructions that Monsieur L'Abbé will give you.

Griffard
I beg Monsieur Desgrez to be with his men on Sunday, before noon, at the Pont St. Denis. What time to you have, Desgrez, by my watch.

Desgrez (pulling out his watch)
This here?

Griffard
Yes.

Desgrez
Ten five, monsieur.

(Desgrez begins to return the watch to his pocket.)

La Reynie
Desgrez, give the watch back to the gentleman.

Desgrez
Here.

Griffard
You rewind it?

Desgrez
Every night.

Griffard
Thanks. Then at ten o'clock, right.

Desgrez
That's all?

Griffard
That's all. If the Lieutenant General will give me my

leave?

La Reynie
Go, Abbé, go, and be careful.

(Desgrez whispers in La Reynie's ear as Griffard takes his hat. Griffard sees this action.)

Griffard
Oh, no, useless, monsieur, useless.

La Reynie (surprised)
What is it?

Griffard
What Monsieur Desgrez proposes—to have me followed.

La Reynie
Plague, Desgrez. Monsieur L'Abbé is strong. He has a fine ear.

Desgrez (to La Reynie, in a low voice)
And where does this gentleman come from?

La Reynie
The galleys.

Griffard (in the doorway, ready to leave)
Escapee.

Desgrez (bowing to him)
O, in that case, Monsieur.

CURTAIN

ACT II

The Fortune Teller

Paris, Rue Beauregard, at La Voisin's home. The first floor is covered with Flanders tapestries, with birds and flowers. In the rear, a little antechamber three steps from the door on the left. On the right, facing the public, a large and high window. To the left a little door with a big bolt. Aspect of a rich and gay bourgeois. To the right a bench and armchair. One can see gardens and tables bordered by a balustrade giving on the Boulevard St. Denis. To the right, several men and women are seated, talking.

(Madame Lamperier and Madame de Feuardent are seated to the right, talking with D'Estrées. Le Gallois is also present. In the rear Guibourg, with his back turned to the room, talks with two bourgeois seated on the bench to the left. There are four groups in the garden.)

Madame Lamperier
Beautiful ceremony, wasn't it?

Madame de Feuardent
Naturally. All the court was there.

Le Gallois
You are speaking of the marriage?

Madame de Feuardent
Of Mademoiselle Colbert and of some nephew of Madame de Montespan, the little Vivonne.

Madame Lamperier
What was the bride wearing?

Madame de Feuardent
All in black velour, sewn with pearls. After dinner with Monsieur Colbert, they were taken to Paris where they were separated because of their age—the husband is fifteen and the wife thirteen.

D'Estrées
She's keeping us waiting a bit, that fortune teller.

Madame Lamperier
It's always better to make an appointment in advance.

Le Gallois
You've already consulted her?

Madame Lamperier
Yes, about a coachman.

D'Estrées
She meddles with that, too?

Madame Lamperier
With everything! Marriages, births, law suits, judgments, loans. It's nothing for her to furnish you with good servants.

De Dommeyrac
Who told her?

Madame de Feuardent
Oh, you joke about everything. What are you doing at La Voisin's?

De Dommeyrac
I just came to see how far human credulity goes.

Madame Lamperier
Consult her. You will be astounded.

D'Estrées (pointing to Guibourg)
Excuse me. Who is that big fellow with a bald head and grey hair?

Madame de Feuardent
It's The Abbé Guibourg, a familiar of this place, like the other one in the reddish wig, Mr. Lesage, the astrologer.

De Dommeyrac
And necromancer.

Madame de Feuardent
You laugh—but that doesn't prevent him from being on good terms with the sibyls.

D'Estrées
The ancient sibyls.

Madame de Feuardent
Yes.

D'Estrées
The same?

Madame de Feuardent and Madame Lamperier
The same!

Madame de Feuardent
You ask them, by letter, whatever you want. Lesage seals the letter and burns it before your eyes.

Madame Lamperier
And you will find it in your home the next day.

Madame de Feuardent
With the response from the sibyls.

(Lesage leaves with Guibourg by the garden.)

D'Estrées (to De Dommeyrac)
You believe all this?

De Dommeyrac
By God, he conjured it away.

(Two ladies leave the room, second from the left.)

Le Gallois
Tell me, don't you find it smells a little burnt here?

Madame de Feuardent (getting up)
Oh! She is at her best with the Curé de Bonne Nouvelle, her parish priest, The Abbé of Sainte-Amour, and the Rector of the University.

(Madame de Feuardent goes towards the door from which clients are exiting with the hope of taking their place. D'Estrées, Le Gallois and de Dommeyrac follow.)

Madame Lamperier
A holy man.

(Marguerite comes out of her mother's room.)

Marguerite
Ladies and gentlemen. My mother begs you to excuse her. She won't receive anyone else.

(General protest. All turn toward Marguerite.)

Le Gallois
I have been here more than an hour.

All
We, too.

Madame Lamperier
It isn't right to make us wait.

Madame de Feuardent
It's indecent.

(General approval, etc.)

Marguerite
Mamma deplores this more than you, but she is tired and cannot do her duty. If these ladies wish to wait on the terrace, they will be offered refreshments there.

De Dommeyrac
Only the ladies?

(Laughter.)

Marguerite
The gentlemen, too.

All (chattering and pushing each other to leave by the door in the back)
About time! Oh! Well! Etc.

Madame de Feuardent (low, to Marguerite, slipping her some money)
Tomorrow, get me in first.

Madame Lamperier (same action)
Me, too.

(All go out with murmurs of confused conversation. They can be seen on the terrace. Two lackeys in livery bring in liquors, wine, fruit, and cake.)

Marguerite (to Margot)
Draw the curtains. (when all the curtains are drawn) You can come in.

Voisin (in the doorway)
Gone?

Marguerite
All!

(Voisin enters. She has on a rob of a sea-green velvet, trimmed with gold. On her head, a diadem of gold. In her hand a gold wand like fairies. She divests herself of her dress with the aid of two girls.)

Marguerite
They complain, you know.

Voisin (putting her wand on the table)
Good, good, let them complain! If they weren't made to wait, they wouldn't come back! Oof! Get me out of this, I am suffocating.

(Margot and Marguerite detach the cloak and diadem and

take them into the room.)

Voisin
Give me a little Angevin wine, Margot.

Margot
Yes, Madame.

Voisin
You gave them something to drink?

Marguerite
Yes! Especially some liquors. They only like that! Here's the list of those who come and will come again.

(Voisin sits in the chair at the right of the table and looks at her list, while Margot enters with a bottle of wine and glasses which she places on the table.)

Voisin (reading)
The Count de Clermont-Lodève!

Marguerite
He will return tomorrow.

Voisin
Oh, every day, and he wants more each time, that one. The death of his brother and the love of his sister-in-law. (reading) Toulousain?

Marguerite
Who didn't wish to give his name. He wanted to cut the throat of his wife's lover.

Voisin
Madame de Poulaillon.

Marguerite
She only came to tell me it's done.

Voisin
Her husband?

Marguerite
Yes! She is radiant! She will come tomorrow to settle the account.

Voisin
I indeed hope it. (reading) Madame Ferrez.

(The bell rings.)

Voisin
They're ringing.

Marguerite
At the dressmaker's. (going to the door) It's a friend. Look, Mademoiselle Desoeillets.

Voisin
Let her come in.

(Marguerite draws the bolt and opens the door.)

Desoeillets (in the doorway)
Alone?

Voisin
Alone! (to Margot) Watch the doors carefully. (going to Desoeillets) The Marquise sent you?

Mademoiselle Desoeillets
Better than that. She's coming.

Voisin
You are sure you weren't followed?

Mademoiselle Desoeillets
No! Before she said, I'm not going to Paris so as not to upset the King about the motives for this trip. Now he doesn't give a damn.

Voisin
You've reached that point?

Mademoiselle Desoeillets
We've reached that point. Yesterday there was a great quarrel between the King and the Marquise over La Fontanges. That's why she's seeking your help as she always does in great crises.

Voisin
And with success, I am proud to boast.

Mademoiselle Desoeillets
Also, I saw someone coming who must be allowed in. Warn Margot.

Voisin
Margot! (Margot returns, to Mademoiselle Desoeillets) How can she be recognized?

Mademoiselle Desoeillets
She's wearing red silk, with green brocade.

Voisin (to Margot)
You hear? You will receive this person. She alone.

Margot
Fine, Madame.

(Margot goes back.)

Voisin (to Mademoiselle Desoeillets)
Who is she?

Mademoiselle Desoeillets
It's Mademoiselle D'Ormoize, a lady of honor to La Fontanges.

Voisin
Ah, fine.

Mademoiselle Desoeillets
She loves the Chevalier de Tralage, the secretary to Ma-

dame de Maintenon. Since she entered Mademoiselle de Fontanges' service, the Chevalier has been neglecting her for her mistress Mademoiselle de Fontanges.

Voisin
Ah! Ah!

Mademoiselle Desoeillets
Mademoiselle D'Ormoize certainly knows what's going on. She has come to consult you. I believe—

Voisin
I will make her talk.

Mademoiselle Desoeillets
Judge what an advantage we will have over our rival when we can prove she's unfaithful to the King.

Voisin
And who will serve us better than this young girl?

Mademoiselle Desoeillets
Confess her. We will see, later. I am going to disappear.

(Mademoiselle Desoeillets goes to the door by which she came and leaves.)

Voisin
Till later.

Mademoiselle Desoeillets (outside)
Yes.

(La Voisin closes the door and puts the bolt in. Just then, three women enter with Solange. Margot goes quickly to bar the way to the others while letting Solange pass.)

Margot
Ladies, it is very late! Madame has closed her door.

Voisin (turning and seeing Solange)
It's she!

(While Margot gently gets rid of the others, Voisin goes to Solange.)

Voisin
You wish, Madame?

Solange (timidly)
I would like to speak to Madame Voisin.

Voisin
That's me. But I don't receive at this hour.

Solange
Pardon! I will come back, Madame.

(Solange takes a step back.)

Voisin (agreeably)
Oh, well, since you are here.

Solange
I thank you, Madame. I heard you highly praised.

Voisin (making her sit in a chair)
Sit down, child, and tell me your trouble. Because, you have trouble, right? A great shame.

Solange (very moved)
Ah, God, if that were possible!

Voisin (taking Solange's hand and inspecting it)
Yes, this hand. Oh, how you tremble. This hand indicates a great, great deception. A pain in your heart, isn't it?

Solange
Yes, oh, yes, that's it!

Voisin
You wish to know if some hope remains to you?

Solange
Yes.

Voisin
We are going to see. The other hand, if you please, and look at me—eye to eye. Oh, they've wept, those eyes! Yes! I read it as in a mirror. A lover, right? A handsome man, yes. At Court! Oh, poor thing, what I see. Yes, you

have given him bounties, very great bounties.

(Solange responds by drying her eyes.)

Solange
Tell me the truth, Madame! Tell me, I want to know. It's over, isn't it? Completely over? He no longer loves me?

Voisin
Wait—not so fast! Oh, my God. This line here—this line is not broken completely.

Solange (excitedly)
Oh, he loves me a little still, a little?

Voisin
But, yes! Only— Ah! Here, between you—a woman! Oh, funny hair, it is red.

Solange
Almost.

Voisin
A coquette! Oh! Very dangerous. Oh, what a coquette she is! And yet, in a situation in which she ought not to compromise herself. But who shines forth? A woman, such a great lady.

Solange
And so pretty, so celebrated, so praised! Between her and a poor girl like me—he cannot hesitate. Every day I feel

he's withdrawing from me more and more, and I, I love him more than ever. I pretend to see nothing. I hide my shame, it's cowardice. I know it, but I am afraid he would use my reproaches to throw me over completely. I prefer to pretend I know nothing to hold him a little longer—for as long as possible—then, afterwards. Ah, God! What will become of me? (crying) I am so—so unhappy.

Voisin
Poor child. You mustn't despair like that. Nothing is lost.

Solange
Oh! There is a little hope—tell me! He will come back to me.

Voisin
First, I must know what I don't see very well.

Solange
What?

Voisin
Has he obtained everything from her?

Solange (quickly)
Oh, that. No!

Voisin
You are sure?

Solange
Oh, yes! Yes! I've been watching very carefully.

Voisin
Who knows?

Solange
Oh! When one loves, one cannot be deceived.

Voisin
Then we must struggle, my dear child. And for that I have wonderful secrets.

Solange
Ah!

Voisin
One especially, which can detach him from this woman and bring him back to you, more tender than ever.

Solange
Ah, God, if it was possible. What is it, Madame? speak!

Voisin
It's a powder!

Solange
A powder?

Voisin
Yes! For love! A powder which must be mixed with some

drink—for your mistress.

Solange
Oh! If this is going to make her ill—

Voisin
No danger!

Solange
Oh, no! No! Oh, I couldn't do that!

Voisin
But—

Solange
No, I wouldn't dare. For myself, I would risk it, but for her—

Voisin
Still—

Solange
No. Give me something for myself.

Voisin
It only acts on her!

Solange
Then, Madame, another way.

Voisin
It's only that which can act on her will.

Solange
But to act on her will by such a means is not permitted.

Voisin
But, yes!

Solange
Oh! No! I am sure of it. It is by magic—you see. It's not Christian.

Voisin (rising)
Oh! Well, my dear, if that's how you feel—

Solange (following her)
Please understand!

Voisin
No! No, let's not speak any more about it.

Solange
Oh! Yes, I much prefer to be patient, to wait, and suffer more.

Voisin
That's it. Let us wait! And let us suffer!

Solange
Pardon me. I am irritating you. What must I do, madame?

Voisin
Nothing! For the moment, only when you return!

Solange
Oh! Never! Adieu, Madame. (goes to the garden and sees Hector) Oh, someone that I wish to avoid and who has seen me.

Voisin (drawing the bolt and opening the little door)
Leave this way.

Solange
Thank you, Madame, thank you. Goodbye, Madame, goodbye.

Voisin
No. Until we meet again.

(Voisin closes the door and bolts it after Solange. At the same time Hector enters, followed by the Duke de Vendome, the Duchess de Bouillon, the Princess de Tingry, and Monsieur de Cessac.)

Margot (trying to block their passage)
Ladies and gentlemen—you cannot go in.

Hector
Madame! The Duchess de Bouillon, de Tingry, the Duke de Vendome, Monsieur de Cessac, and your servant wish to consult you.

Voisin
Too late, monsieur. At this time I am good for nothing! I pray these ladies will excuse me. (going)

Hector (stopping her)
A word, pardon! The lady who just left— (pointing to the door) Wasn't it Mademoiselle D'Ormoize?

Voisin
I don't know, monsieur. She didn't give her name.

(Voisin goes to the ladies and speaks to them.)

Hector (to de Cessac)
Cessac, it really was D'Ormoize, wasn't it?

De Cessac
It seemed so to me.

Hector (to himself)
What's she coming here for?

De Cessac
She came to have her fortune told.

Hector
And you, I bet—to ask how to win at gambling with certainty.

(De Cessac sees Lesage leave Voisin's room with his hat under his arm.)

De Cessac
You said it! Ah, here's my man. (confronting Lesage) Ah, the gentleman rogue, I have some business with you.

Lesage (bowing)
Sir, you surprise me.

De Cessac
You recognize me, I think.

Lesage (bowing again)
When one has had the honor to see Monsieur—

De Cessac
It is I who asked you a week ago for a secret of how to always win at gambling.

Lesage
Exactly, monsieur.

De Cessac
You told me that if you had such a secret you would keep it for yourself.

Hector (laughing)
By God!

De Cessac
You told me only a charlatan could boast of knowing it. But instead of that, you added, you would give me a coin that no matter how I lost it would return to my pocket.

Hector
Oh! Oh!

Lesage (to de Cessac)
Yes, monsieur! It's a flying coin.

De Cessac
Well, I bought your flying coin. I lost it yesterday, and I am still waiting for it

Lesage
And it hasn't returned?

De Cessac
No, monsieur! No.

Lesage
It's very astonishing! There must be some reason. Ah! I have it! Aren't we in a quarter-moon?

De Cessac
I don't know.

Hector
Yes!

Lesage
There. That explains everything. It cannot return until a full moon.

De Cessac
Ah!

Hector
Didn't he tell you that?

De Cessac
No.

Lesage
An oversight. At the full moon, monsieur, at the full moon. Not before!

(Lesage bows and leaves at the back.)

De Cessac (to Hector, who laughs)
You don't believe it?

Hector
As to his flying coin—no. But as to your stolen coins—yes.

(De Cessac and Hector leave by the right. Griffard enters the way Lesage left. Marguerite runs to Griffard to prevent him from entering.)

Marguerite
Eh! Monsieur! Monsieur! Mama isn't receiving any more.

Griffard
This little girl is sweet. You are going to see, honey, that

she will receive me.

Marguerite
But, monsieur—

Griffard
I am coming about an inheritance.

Marguerite
Yes?

Griffard
Hers. Hmm, not even a stuffed owl. No sign of deviltry here.

Marguerite
An inheritance! Oh, then, in that case. Eh, mama! Mama!

(Marguerite goes out and returns with Voisin.)

Voisin
An inheritance?

Marguerite
Yes.

Voisin (seeing Griffard)
An Abbé! I understand. The legacy of a dying person. Everyone is gone. Draw the curtains. (to Griffard) Ah, monsieur priest. Sit down, I beg you. Tell me quickly from whom have I inherited.

Griffard (smiling)
My dear Madame, you know it better than I.

Voisin
No.

Griffard
You are mocking. A fortune teller who reads in rumors, in coffee, on hands!

Voisin
Yes, but—

Griffard
Come, come, read these, very quickly—who I am and from where I come and about what business.

Voisin
Impossible. From the moment it concerns me, I lose all my ability.

Griffard (laughing)
Cheater!

Voisin (stunned)
You say?

Griffard (winking at her)
Cheater! Carloni told me you were.

Voisin
Carloni?

Griffard (mysteriously)
It's from him you inherit.

Voisin
Dead?

Griffard
In my arms.

Voisin
At sea?

Griffard
On dry land. He escaped with me.

Voisin
Oh! You were—

Griffard
Comrades of the galley.

Voisin
Oh, tell me then—what do I inherit?

Griffard
From the trunk.

Voisin (pretending not to understand)
The trunk?

Griffard
Down in your garden, behind the bench.

Voisin
Ah, you know.

Griffard
Naturally, I inherit with you.

Voisin
I don't get all?

Griffard
Greedy!

Voisin (defiant)
Hum! You say that, but first of all, what is in that trunk? I don't know at all.

Griffard
Let's refresh your memory! A thousand ducats in pure gold.

Voisin
And who can prove to me that you get a share?

Griffard
Half—exactly. If he left it all to you, he would have told

me nothing.

Voisin
Hum! He didn't sign some paper for you?

Griffard
On the grand highway! Must one also remind you of where this money come from?

Voisin
My word! It was so long ago.

Griffard (in her ear)
It was for his role in poisoning the Duke of Savoy.

Voisin (shocked)
He told you that?

Griffard
Nothing hidden from me—the good Carloni.

Voisin
It would have been better, after all, to leave me the larger share.

Griffard
Come on! Don't cheat me of mine. (indicating the room and furnishings) You have enough business.

Voisin
Enough, yes.

Griffard

What luxury! Madame has, it seems, lackeys, carriages and an open table.

Voisin

It's necessary for business! But also I have trouble enough. Go! Think that every living day I have consultations from three to seven and sometimes in the morning, without counting séances in town.

Griffard

To read fortunes.

Voisin

The past, the future, all! At nine years old I told cards on the bridges. It is there that I met and married Monsieur Montvoisin who was a mercer on the Pont Marie.

Griffard

And where is he, Montvoisin?

Voisin

At Meudon with the gout. He's a bear! And since I became a wise woman, I have rendered services in this condition.

Griffard

I believe it. And now you have become a sorceress.

Voisin

You can say that! I read in the stars. With this, I sell talismans, philters, secrets for women's toilet, a water of my making, The Argentine. I don't need to tell you this! And also remedies for illnesses.

Griffard
Which you cure?

Voisin
Yes.

Griffard
That you create?

Voisin (gaily)
That, too! One must create what the clients desire, especially the women.

Griffard
Who, for instance?

Voisin
Oh, never the names! That's the secret of the job. But without telling the names, if you saw them coming here to me—Ooh la la! And what they ask!

Griffard
What more?

Voisin
Oh! wealth, to inherit as soon as possible from papa, mama, etc., to win at gambling, to find treasures, to not get

fat, to not get old, and almost all—to be relieved of their husbands in order to marry their lovers.

Griffard
And for this, the best way?

Voisin
Damn!

Griffard
Aren't you afraid?

Voisin
Of what?

Griffard
Of the police?

Voisin
Oh—I laugh at the police. There are too many more interesting people for them to cause me trouble.

Griffard
And then, aren't you afraid the devil will carry you off?

Voisin
You can laugh, but I count on him.

Griffard
You believe in him, the devil?

Voisin
If I do?

Griffard
You have seen him?

Voisin
No! But one doesn't see God. That doesn't prevent you from believing in him.

Griffard
Ah, you believe in God, too?

Voisin
In God? What a question! And you?

Griffard
Sometimes! But, how can you be on good terms with both of them at the same time?

Voisin
To each his role! I go to mass and vespers on Sunday. I confess and commune twice a year. I fast Friday. What more can God ask of me?

Griffard
Not to do what he forbids.

Voisin
Ah, well—if one only did what he permits—people would be too bored. It's only with the other one who amuses

himself and makes good business—and he is the stronger of the two. Go!

Griffard
You will be damned!

Voisin
Good! One has only to repent at the last minute like Brinvilliers and God will forgive. He's there for that! But you make me chatter so. And you? Do you want something to drink? (going to table) Why were you there?

Griffard
For counterfeiting.

Voisin
That gives more trouble than profit.

Griffard
Which is why I've given it up and am preparing a big deal.

Voisin
What?

Griffard
It's—you will keep it secret?

Voisin
Yes, yes.

Griffard (lowering his voice)
It's the death of the King.

Voisin (quickly turning to him)
You, too?

Griffard
Too? Someone else has proposed it to you?

Voisin
That deal—yes, it will pay richly. A hundred thousand crowns, I only wait for that to retire from business.

Griffard
Can it be for the same people?

Voisin (near him)
Who are you doing it for?

Griffard
Oh! I won't beat around the bush. For the friends of Monsieur Fouquet.

Voisin (quickly)
Me, too!

Griffard
Who, giving up on his pardon, can see only the death of the King as a way of getting him out of prison.

Voisin
That's it. They are three.

Griffard
One who has a false eye.

Voisin
Monsieur de Martroy!

Griffard
No, not him, a little smaller.

Voisin
The auditor of accounts, Maillard.

Griffard
Maillard, yes. So, for the third—I am sure he gave me a false name.

Voisin
Isn't he named La Brosse?

Griffard
Who knows? I only know these three.

Voisin
Then, you've met them?

Griffard
All the time.

Voisin
And the dogs have offered you—

Griffard
Yes!

Voisin
After having offered it to me?

Griffard
They found you were too slow.

Voisin
It is so easy, isn't it? At the King's table, the dishes and wines are tasted in advance—and his plate is under a cover of which only he and the taster have the key.

Griffard
There's still a way to get it to him. Some day, when hunting, for example, in a woods, in the water—

Voisin
And still, one must have an accomplice.

Griffard
I have one.

Voisin
Oh, who?

Griffard
I am going to tell you so you can ruin my business?

Voisin
Oh! No! Between friends. (suddenly) But, instead of disputing, let's do it together.

Griffard
Not stupid, you! What do you bring to it?

Voisin
The poison.

Griffard (laughing)
Thanks! Some apothecary's drug.

Voisin
You have something better?

Griffard
Me? I have the best of all—the true—the only—

Voisin
Oh! What?

Griffard
That of the Borgias.

Voisin (with admiration)
Oh, yes—that—

Griffard
You will tell me news of it.

Voisin (coming to him)
Oh, my honey! It would be so nice for us to work together.

Griffard
Phooey!

Voisin
Not for that, alone, no! For everything! (he looks at her) Yes, I am rich, you know. (she sits on the arm of Griffard's chair and puts her arm around his neck) With all the money I've got put aside, the money from this business—and the money in that trunk in the ground—I will buy land in the provinces—where we will go plant our cabbages, you and I, Abbé of my heart, for you please me. You have no idea how you please me. We will live like lords. Wouldn't you like it? Tell me, my big darling honey.

Griffard
Eh! My God.

Voisin
Then, it's agreed?

Griffard
Give me time.

Voisin
It's agreed. And to begin, you are going to sup with me.

Griffard (starting)
To sup?

Voisin
What's wrong with you?

Griffard
You just reminded me that I was invited to sup with Martroy and Maillard—to discuss this business.

Voisin
Well, sup with them, and come back and sleep here.

Griffard
Oh! We will have to spend the entire night preparing the Borgia. Tomorrow, rather.

Voisin
For dinner, then?

Griffard
Yes! Oh, tomorrow, whenever you like.

Voisin
Ah! Lovely man! How sweet you are. I am going to go crazy about you! Wait! I adore you. (she kisses him, then rises at the sight of Guibourg appearing in the garden with Margot and Marguerite) Don't budge! It's a friend.

Griffard (standing, wiping off his mouth)
Yuck!

Voisin (calling)
Guibourg! (low to Griffard) Not a word about the trunk or the King! (aloud) The Abbé Guibourg. The Abbé Griffard who came to tell me of the death of the poor Carloni with whom he escaped from the galleys.

(Griffard takes his hat from the table.)

Marguerite and Margot
Dead!

Guibourg
Poor fellow.

Voisin (looking around)
Lesage isn't here?

Marguerite
Left!

Voisin (to Guibourg)
Without telling me! The imbecile! I had need of him.

(The bell rings.)

Marguerite
Someone's ringing.

(Marguerite runs quickly to the door at the left.)

Voisin
Don't open it. (Marguerite stops) Close the curtains. (to Griffard who seems about to go) No, no—stay—I will tell you why—go in there. (pointing to her room) It's a person who must not be seen, even masked.

Griffard
Ah, who then?

Voisin
A beauty of the court who wishes to supplant two rivals.

Griffard (curious)
But, still?

Voisin
Hush! Go there, with Guibourg. You can kill time playing cards! He's a great card player.

Griffard
He looks it. We'll play chess.

Voisin (to Margot)
Give them something to drink.

Griffard
No, never between meals.

(They go out.)

Marguerite (to her mother)
Who is that man?

Voisin
An intriguer that I interest. He will ruin the death of the King if I am not quicker than he. Tomorrow morning, early, Margot will go tell Monsieur de Martroy (ringing) that I will wait for him all day and that I am on fire to see him. Open.

(Marguerite draws the bolt and opens the door.)

Mademoiselle Desoeillets (in the doorway)
She's there—getting impatient.

(She goes to introduce the Marquise.)

Voisin (stopping her)
We must get rid of everyone else. (low) Mademoiselle D'Ormoize came.

Mademoiselle Desoeillets (stopping)
Well?

Voisin
A goose! Nothing doing.

(Mademoiselle Desoeillets shrugs, then in a low voice addresses the Marquise who is unseen.)

Mademoiselle Desoeillets
If Madame wishes to enter— (the Marquise enters, masked) I will return in an hour.

(Mademoiselle Desoeillets leaves. Voisin locks the door behind her. Madame de Montespan sits down and looks around.)

Madame de Montespan
We are alone?

Voisin
Alone, Madame, and the doors are closed.

Madame de Montespan (unmasking, very upset)
Voisin—it's me again! Always me! You see a woman in despair.

Voisin
Yes, Mademoiselle Desoeillets told me.

Madame de Montespan
Yesterday, the King found a way to quarrel with me over this doll he is mad about.

Voisin
La Fontanges?

Madame de Montespan
A scene! Because I refused to admire the silly way she dances. Everyone was laughing behind their fans. I cried

all night.

Voisin
Poor Madame.

Madame de Montespan
Ah! Voisin, the King is resolved to break with me over her. He doesn't love me anymore.

Voisin
Dear Madame, you have said that so often.

Madame de Montespan
This time I am not mistaken. God! My reign is finished.

Voisin
No indeed, no indeed.

Madame de Montespan
Oh, yes, and for a creature I had the stupidity to throw in his arms myself.

Voisin
You?

Madame de Montespan
Yes. I told myself that since he must always have new fresh fruit, this King, well, rather this one than another. She is nothing, this girl—and through a bitter stupidity I led her to him, expecting to reign longer under her name while she lasted.

Voisin
And then?

Madame de Montespan
Then? She's been ungrateful to me—insolent. He's offered me the post of Superintendent of the Queen's household.

Voisin
Proof he still loves you.

Madame de Montespan
Not at all. It's to give me a job that will give him more freedom. Still, I don't worry that much about La Fontanges.

Voisin
Well then?

Madame de Montespan
Madame Maintenon. Another work of mine.

Voisin
That's true.

Madame de Montespan
I forced the King to make her the governess of our children, despite his dislike of her. How could I have foreseen how the little hypocrite, widow of a cripple, would ensnare him with her pretended maternal cares. Oh, I understood her too late. A whipper of children! A dishrag.

Voisin
Is she really so clever?

Madame de Montespan
Ah. Oh, if you saw her dressed as if she were in mourning, sitting in her corner like a spider.

Voisin
Well, Madame, you must fight.

Madame de Montespan
That's why I again have recourse to your enchantments.

Voisin
There is only one, Madame, one alone—which you have always refused. The Black Mass and the powders.

Madame de Montespan
Yes!

Voisin
We've said others, and they were successful.

Madame de Montespan
Yes! They were great triumphs.

Voisin
Then, you have no reason to doubt my power—

Madame de Montespan
No! But this Mass, can't you do it, as we did twice, with

Mademoiselle Desoeillets taking my place.

Voisin
No. This time your presence is indispensable.

Madame de Montespan (sickened, turning her head away)
It is so unpleasant.

Voisin
Consider, you can wear your mask and no one will know who you are except my daughter and myself.

Madame de Montespan
Are you sure?

Voisin
Oh, who would think it you? Your name has never been mentioned.

Madame de Montespan
But! Who will say the Mass?

Voisin
The same as always, The Abbé Guibourg.

Madame de Montespan
And Lesage?

Voisin
And Lesage—for servant. (insisting) Madame—

Madame de Montespan
Then so be it. If it must be.

Voisin
Absolutely.

Madame de Montespan
But, where and when?

Voisin
But here, Madame. Right away.

Madame de Montespan
Is it possible?

Voisin
I foresaw this. (calling) Marguerite! (to Madame de Montespan) We will need a night to prepare the powders after the ceremony. My daughter will bring them to you.

(Marguerite enters.)

Voisin (to Marguerite)
Go prepare everything above!

(Marguerite nods and goes out.)

Voisin
Madame still has this wine taster of the King's at her command?

Madame de Montespan
Gillot, yes.

Voisin
He will put the powders in the King's right night stand.

Madame de Montespan
Yes, in the orangeade the King likes at night.

Voisin
If Madame will go with Marguerite.

Madame de Montespan
My mask! Oh, how happy Madame de Maintenon would be if she could see what she forces me to do.

(Madame de Montespan puts her mask back on and goes into the room.)

Voisin
Enter! Enter!

Griffard
And it works like checkers. (to Voisin) Where is the lady?

Voisin
Hush! Up there! (pointing to her room) I was right to keep you here. You are going to replace Lesage.

Griffard
To do what?

Voisin
To assist in the Black Mass we are going to say.

Griffard
The Black Mass? Are people still engaging in such deviltry?

Voisin
You know what it is?

Griffard
Not well.

Voisin
This will inform you.

Griffard
Good! My role will be?

Voisin (taking a candelabra from the table and giving it to Margot)
Nothing to do, except to enter with me with a candle in your hand and place it behind the masked lady who will be stretched out. She won't see your face and will take you for Lesage. Not a word that will betray you. When everything is finished, blow out your candle and leave quickly. We won't need you to prepare the powders tonight.

Griffard
And will this last long?

Voisin
You won't find it long. (Marguerite reappears) It's ready and here is Guibourg!

(Guibourg comes out of La Voisin's chamber, dressed in black. He is followed by Margot carrying two black candles. They go into the chamber.)

Griffard
Ah! This is Guibourg?

Voisin
Who officiates, yes.

(Voisin takes the candles from Margot's hand.)

Voisin
Take this. (giving Griffard a candle) Follow me.

Griffard
Guibourg and I—two Abbés! If the devil isn't happy.

Voisin (to Margot)
Watch carefully, you!

Margot
Oh, Madame—I have a sharp eye.

(Voisin leaves and closes the door. Margot runs to watch through the keyhole.)

CURTAIN

ACT III

The Grotto of Thetis

The Grotto of Thetis at Versailles, lighted by candles. In the back, groups by Girardon and de Marsy, behind which is the orchestra. Doors on the sides with grills. Those on the left giving on the park, on the right to the palace. Two pillars in the fore scene. To the right rear buffets, chairs. Groups of courtiers coming and going, rising, sitting and talking. To the left a group of three ladies seated, de Brionne and D'Estrées standing.

De Dommeyrac (bowing to de Brionne)
Is this the first time a concert has been given in the grotto?

De Brionne
Yes, I believe so. (to D'Estrées) Right?

D'Estrées
The first.

De Brionne
Here is the program.

(The distributor of the programs, a Negro in costume, gives them some programs which they pass to the ladies.)

First Lady (reading)
Lulli, March of Bacchus, Bellerophon—

D'Estrées
The success of the day.

Second Lady
The Italian complaint—Psyche.

(Colbert appears in the back, coming from the right. He comes forward and bows and is bowed to. The Negro gives him a program. He sees De Visé at the right who bows profoundly to him.)

Colbert
Monsieur De Visé, this little festivity will occupy six pages at least of your Mercury.

De Visé
Monsieur Colbert deigns to do it the honor of reading it.

Colbert
With bitterness.

De Visé
That is the sweetest reward.

De Dommeyrac (in a low voice to the ladies at the sight of Louvois who bows and is bowed to)
The Marquis de Louvois.

Colbert (to Louvois, bowing)
Monsieur the Marquis.

Louvois
Monsieur!

D'Estrées (to the ladies at the sight of Lulli)
Monsieur Lulli.

Lulli (to Louvois)
If Monsieur the Marchese de Louvois deigns to accept his humble servant?

Louvois
And where are your musicians, Monsieur Lulli?

Lulli
Behind the statues, Monsieur Marchese, so the music sounds like it comes from heaven.

Louvois
Ah, fine, fine.

(Lulli goes back. Madame de Montespan comes in with Mademoiselle Desoeillets, Madame d'Humières, Madame de Brissac, Madame de Nevers, two ladies and courtiers. Many bows.)

Madame de Montespan
It's pretty, this lighted grotto. Isn't it, gentlemen?

Louvois
Madame, I am happy to see you are not suffering as we had feared.

Madame de Montespan
Yesterday, yes, a little migraine. But today—

Colbert
More beautiful than ever.

Madame de Montespan
I regret, gentlemen, to inform you that the Queen, consumed with her devotions, will not appear at the concert.

(Murmurs of deception.)

Madame de Nevers
Here's Madame the Dauphine.

(Coming from the right, appearing in the rear where they remain, Madame and the Dauphine. Then Fontanges, followed by Mademoiselle D'Ormoize. Many bows to the newcomers.)

Colbert (to Madame de Montespan)
And Mademoiselle de Fontanges—very languid—as is usual with her.

(Colbert goes to greet the Dauphine.)

Madame de Montespan
She can hardly walk, the poor girl, and must remain on her chaise longue.

(De Dommeyrac, after having greeted the Dauphine and Madame, returns to Madame de Montespan with de Brionne and D'Estrées.)

De Dommeyrac
Monsieur is more seducing than ever and Madame more manly.

De Brionne
She only lacks a mustache!

Madame de Montespan
And she is too much for Monsieur.

(The three ladies of the Marquise, Mesdames de Brissac, de Nevers and d'Humières, after having quitted the princesses, return and stay to the right of the Marquise.)

Madame de Brissac
I don't see Madame de Maintenon.

Madame de Montespan
Oh, don't wait for her—the Grotto of Thetis irritates her. Hasn't she spoken to me of demolishing it?

(Protestations.)

De Brionne
And why?

Madame de Montespan
Her virtue won't permit the King to play Apollo with all these beauties surrounding him.

De Dommeyrac (seeing Hector in a group at the right)
Tralage there agrees with you. (calling) Chevalier!

(Tralage turns and goes to the Marquise to whom he bows)

Will well have the pleasure of seeing Madame de Maintenon?

Hector
Madame de Maintenon is at her devotions, with the approval of His Majesty.

Madame de Montespan
What did I tell you? (to Hector) Thank you, monsieur.

(Hector bows and goes back.)

De Brionne
A beautiful visit! Maintenon.

De Dommeyrac
Yes, but well paid.

Madame de Montespan
Two hundred thousand crowns! That's the price of a patent that the King has given—the King—and which she sold.

D'Estrées
A Patent?

Madame de Montespan
For an invention!

All
The Marquise?

Madame de Montespan
Eh, yes, a new economical furnace.

(Discreet laughter.)

Madame d'Humières (laughing)
Come on, Madame de Maintenon!

Madame de Montespan
Yes, you can indeed recognize the old household of Monsieur Scarron.

(She goes with those who surround her to greet Fontanges and meets La Reynie coming forward. Meanwhile Griffard enters from the right.)

Madame de Montespan (to La Reynie)
Good day, monsieur.

(She goes to great the princesses.)

La Reynie (seeing The Abbé)
Ah, Monsieur Griffard.

Griffard (bowing)
Monsieur.

La Reynie
I was looking for you.

Griffard
In giving me a pass for the concert, Desgrez told me you wished to meet me here.

La Reynie
Before anything else, my compliments, monsieur. You have done wonders. Come to the side, I beg you.

(They go to the right.)

Griffard
Desgrez has told you?

La Reynie
The arrest of La Voisin and her clique, yes!

Griffard
And the strange ceremony at which I assisted yesterday?

La Reynie
Yes. It appears they hadn't yet had time to remove the traces of that sacrilegious mass.

Griffard
Said at the request of a lady of the court for the removal of her rivals. That was all I could get out of La Voisin.

La Reynie
And you didn't catch the features of this woman?

Griffard
No. She kept her mask on throughout.

La Reynie
She is, perhaps, not two feet from us. Did she see your face?

Griffard
Oh, surely not, monsieur! I was stationed behind her, candle in hand. But when she rose unexpectedly, I let a bit of hot wax from my candle fall on her shoulder.

La Reynie
She cannot recognize you?

Griffard
No more than I can recognize her.

La Reynie
In place of other means, her voice?

Griffard
No word escaped her teeth except "clumsy" when I spilled the wax. All I can say is that she's not in her first youth.

Griffard
She is well made, nice figure. But you will learn quickly from La Voisin who she is.

La Reynie
Doubtless.

Griffard
For me, monsieur, my role is finished. I wish you courage, for you need it with the trouble you've got.

La Reynie
I am worried.

Griffard
What I learned from La Voisin was very upsetting. The King is a great King, but in Versailles there is a bad odor. Behind the splendor, the court knows no morality, devotion or religion except the cult of worshipping the King.

La Reynie
Think of it, but don't speak of it! Don't go far, perhaps I may need you.

Griffard
At your orders, monsieur. Versailles is unaware of this morning's arrest?

La Reynie
It is likely.

Griffard
I am curious to see the effect it will produce. (seeing De Visé) Here's someone coming.

La Reynie
Do it!

(Bowing. De Visé comes forward with D'Estrées, de Brionne, and de Dommeyrac.)

Griffard
My dear De Visé.

De Visé
Ah! It's The Abbé Griffard.

De Brionne (to Griffard)
Resurrected?

De Visé
At the Mercury, they thought you were dead.

Griffard
Only a voyage.

D'Estrées
Business?

Griffard
Right. I just arrived and am hardly installed.

De Visé
At Versailles?

Griffard
At Paris, from which I bring you startling news. The arrest of the popular fortune teller.

All
Voisin?

(The name strikes Mademoiselle Desoeillets, who cups her ear.)

Griffard
Voisin!

(Mademoiselle Desoeillets detaches herself from the other ladies to listen to Griffard without appearing to do so.)

De Visé
And why?

Griffard
For witchcraft and poisons!

Mademoiselle Desoeillets (going to Griffard)
Pardon, Monsieur Abbé—La Voisin arrested, do you say?

Griffard (bowing)
This very morning.

Mademoiselle Desoeillets
Are you sure?

Griffard
I was there.

Mademoiselle Desoeillets
Thank you.

(Mademoiselle Desoeillets goes to find Madame de Montespan.)

Griffard
One of her clients. (to De Visé) Who is she?

De Visé
La Desoeillets.

De Dommeyrac
Lady-in-waiting to Madame de Montespan.

Griffard
Ah!

De Visé
The arrest of La Voisin is going to surprise many people.

Griffard
And distract others.

(Griffard takes a program and reads, but observes. He sees Madame de Montespan and Mademoiselle Desoeillets and the others go off. Madame de Montespan is very upset. Mademoiselle Desoeillets goes to the buffet to get orange-ade for her mistress, but encounters Solange.)

Mademoiselle Desoeillets (to Solange)
Good day, mademoiselle.

Solange
Good day, mademoiselle. (to a lackey who is serving) A cup of iced milk, if you please.

Mademoiselle Desoeillets
For Mademoiselle de Fontanges?

Solange
Yes.

Mademoiselle Desoeillets
She's very pretty—in the dark.

Solange
But, so weak and so suffering.

Mademoiselle Desoeillets
One must always pay for one's happiness.

(Mademoiselle Desoeillets rejoins Madame de Montespan to whom she gives the orangeade while Solange goes to Fontanges.)

Griffard (to a porter)
My friend, you see the Marquise there?

Porter
Yes, monsieur.

Griffard
Here's a pistole for you, if you jostle her chair.

Porter
Oh, monsieur, I wouldn't dare.

Griffard
Two crowns.

Porter
I'll try.

(The porter goes by and jostles her drink which spills.)

Madame de Montespan
Clumsy!

Porter
Pardon, I—

Madame de Montespan (drying her robe)
Go away, imbecile.

Griffard
No doubt about it!

(Griffard goes off.)

Mademoiselle Desoeillets (on her knees, drying Madame de Montespan's dress)
It is nothing.

Madame de Montespan
The booby.

Mademoiselle Desoeillets

Madame is feeling better?

Madame de Montespan
Yes, a little surprised, that's all. I hardly expected such news!

Mademoiselle Desoeillets
We will tell La Voisin to keep her mouth shut and we will save her.

Madame de Montespan
Even if she speaks, no one would believe her. Who would dare to accuse me?

A Voice (in the distance)
The King!

(There is a general stir as the King arrives. Two guards appear before the King and the violins attack the March of Bellerophon. Followed at a distance by Monsieur, then Louvois and Colbert, then ladies, the King appears. He bows to the ladies. Then he goes to the Dauphine, whose hand he kisses, then the Princess. People jostle each other to see what is happening.)

Madame de Montespan (to Mademoiselle Desoeillets)
Look at them, the sluts. They know about our quarrel of yesterday and are watching our meeting to see in what tone he greets me.

(The King comes to Madame de Montespan, makes her a profound bow and kisses her hand.)

King
Too much perfume, Marquise, always too much.

Madame de Montespan
I will ask Madame de Maintenon for the jasmine with which she bewitches you and of which you never complain, Your Majesty.

(The King makes no reply, but turns his back with a light bow and goes toward Fontanges.)

Madame de Montespan (bitterly)
You see!

(The King talks to Fontanges, and takes her hand, then sits beside her. The King raises his cane which is a signal for the concert. The orchestra begins playing "Psyche". Hector, spotting Solange, goes to her.)

Hector (low voice, cautiously)
Solange—

(She trembles, turns, sees him, then goes to him while others watch the King.)

Hector
Let's talk without appearing to, my dear. Was it really you at that woman's who was just arrested?

Solange
Yes.

Hector
And why did you try to avoid me?

Solange
I didn't want to be seen with you.

Hector
Why?

Solange
My God, what can I tell you, Hector? I avoided you by instinct because I was ashamed of my motive in visiting that woman.

Hector
What motive, my dear Solange?

Solange
Why do you ask, Hector? You know very well.

Hector
You came to consult the fortune teller?

Solange
Yes.

Hector
What madness, my poor child! Could you expect a serious revelation from her?

Solange
Oh! She told me many truths.

Hector
Of the past, perhaps, and the present—but what does she know of the future?

Solange
When someone is suffering, it isn't very difficult, especially when she gives one some hope.

Hector
Or some despair.

Solange
Also, yes. One prefers to know the evil that awaits one.

Hector
Well, my dear, it is not to this adventuress you must address yourself, but to me.

Solange
To you?

Hector
I would have been better able than she to give peace to your poor injured heart.

Solange
Oh, Hector.

Hector (taking her hand)
Be assured that that which gives you trouble is not as serious as it appears. It was only a moment of madness—of forgetfulness—of which I am now heartily ashamed. Believe it, dear child, and—

(Scream from Madame d'Humières, who sees La Fontanges faint. Exclamations, etc. The music suddenly stops. Solange runs to Fontanges.)

Hector
What is it?

De Dommeyrac
Mademoiselle de Fontanges is ill.

(The King, Madame, and Madame de Montespan surround La Fontanges.)

King
Everyone, get back a pace. Some distance, ladies, I beg you, some distance.

(The ladies obey.)

Madame de Montespan (to Mademoiselle Desoeillets)
A glass, your salts.

(Madame de Montespan takes salts from Mademoiselle Desoeillets and makes La Fontanges inhale.)

King
D'Aquin, where is d'Aquin?

(Voices call "D'Aquin, d'Aquin." Solange gets on her knees before Fontanges.)

Solange
Madame, dear Madame.

Mademoiselle Desoeillets
Her belt!

(D'Aquin runs in with La Reynie.)

King
See, monsieur, see.

D'Aquin
Give me room, ladies, I beg you. She's sick.

King
Suddenly!

Madame de Montespan
Her health is deplorable.

(D'Aquin bends over Fontanges and takes her pulse.)

Louvois
The heat, perhaps.

Solange
Madame complained of being cold.

D'Aquin
Shivering. (to Fontanges) You suffer a great deal, Madame? (she replies with a gesture) Where do you suffer?

(she indicates her stomach) Here, yes—some cramps? (she replies only by gestures) Yes, violent.

Mademoiselle Desoeillets
Was it this iced milk which Mademoiselle Solange gave to her?

D'Aquin
You gave Madame—?

Solange
At her request, monsieur.

D'Aquin
And, after having drunk it?

Solange
Some minutes after.

D'Aquin
What's necessary is to get Madame to her room quickly.

(Two servants take her chair and carry her out on it. Many go with her.)

D'Aquin
Gently, gently, go! I'll be with you in a moment. (to King) We will give her milk—but warm this time. It's still the best antidote.

King
Then you think—?

D'Aquin
Oh, Sire. There's not much time.

Madame de Montespan
It's exactly the case of Madame after the chicory water.

King (to Solange)
Stay, miss! Where did you get this cup of milk?

Solange
At the buffet, like everybody. (points)

King
The cup didn't leave your hand?

Solange
No, Sire.

D'Aquin
Where is it?

Solange
On this table, monsieur.

(Solange indicates the table behind the pillar on the left and goes to get it, but D'Aquin prevents her. He seizes the cup and examines it. Everyone is watching. D'Aquin gives the cup to the master of the hotel.)

D'Aquin
Let this be kept with care, and be careful not to wash it.

(The master of the hotel takes it and leaves by the right.)

Solange
Oh! What can one think?

King
You are in a great hurry to excuse yourself when no one has accused you.

Solange
But, Sire, Monsieur d'Aquin—

King
Return to your rooms and await my order. (pointing to La Reynie) And those of this gentleman.

Solange
Oh! My God, my God! Me? Is it possible?

(Solange collapses in an armchair in tears.)

King
Ladies, you may retire.

(The King bows and leaves by the right. Colbert and Louvois follow with most of the gentlemen.)

Hector (to La Reynie)
Monsieur, you don't think Mademoiselle D'Ormoize capable?

La Reynie
Spare me, Hector, from replying to you.

Hector
You won't blame me if I accompany her, just to her door.

La Reynie
I will blame you greatly if you don't.

(Hector goes to Solange and, taking her hand, leads her out.)

La Reynie (to Griffard who is seated by the pillar at the right)
Well, Monsieur Griffard, this accident doesn't cause you to reflect any?

Griffard
Pardon me. It's not a crime to give iced milk to a sick person.

La Reynie
Nothing else?

Griffard
Nothing.

La Reynie
It doesn't seem to you that the unknown last night might be—

Griffard
Mademoiselle D'Ormoize? No, monsieur, great God, no. It was neither her voice, nor—

La Reynie
I still have reason to believe Mademoiselle D'Ormoize very hostile to her mistress.

Griffard
I know nothing about that. But I know very well that the woman of the Black Mass wasn't this young girl.

La Reynie
We will see, indeed, we will see!

(La Reynie leaves by the right.)

Madame de Montespan (to Mademoiselle Desoeillets)
Call your brother. Have him bring our chairs. We will return to Clagny.

Griffard (to De Visé)
Well, dear friend!

De Visé
What an adventure.

Griffard (loud)
Yes, the milk was thought to be poisoned, thanks to La Voisin.

De Visé
And to think, we were with her, innocently.

Griffard
I, too—

(Madame de Montespan listens. Mademoiselle Desoeillets returns with her cloak. Madame de Montespan makes a sign to be quiet.)

De Visé
Yesterday.

Griffard
In the evening.

Madame de Montespan (low)
Listen!

Griffard
And this morning, I was one of the first to visit a room in disorder, where there had been a certain ceremony.

Madame de Montespan (to Mademoiselle Desoeillets)
This man knows too much. Let him come here.

De Visé
What ceremony?

Griffard
Imagine.

Mademoiselle Desoeillets (interrupting)
Pardon, Monsieur Abbé.

Griffard (rising)
Mademoiselle.

(The others rise and form new groups.)

Mademoiselle Desoeillets
Madame the Marquise would like to speak to you.

Griffard (coming)
Very honored.

(Griffard goes to the Marquise.)

Madame de Montespan
Thank you, monsieur. I have the pleasure of speaking to The Abbé—

Griffard
Griffard, Madame, The Abbé Griffard, at your feet.

Madame de Montespan
I beg you to have a seat. You were talking about some-

thing which interests me. I heard you speaking of this sorceress—La Voisin is her name, right?

Griffard
La Voisin is her name. Yes, Madame.

Madame de Montespan
I think you were saying you had seen traces of some ceremony at her place?

Griffard
The Black Mass.

Madame de Montespan (teasingly)
Do such things really exist?

Griffard
Indeed, yes, Madame. Indeed, yes. In fact, I am sure of it.

Madame de Montespan
Really! Do you hear, Mademoiselle Desoeillets?

Mademoiselle Desoeillets
Yes, Madame.

Madame de Montespan
And how can you be sure?

Griffard
Through the witnessing of a friend who assisted at one of them, in fact, precisely the one in question.

(Mademoiselle Desoeillets and Madame de Montespan tremble.)

Madame de Montespan (troubled)
Your friend must have been joking.

Griffard
Why?

Madame de Montespan (forgetting herself)
Because there were only two officiants.

(Mademoiselle Desoeillets motions to warn her.)

Griffard
Did I say there were only two?

Madame de Montespan
Everyone knows there are only two.

Griffard
Exactly. The usual servant, a certain Lesage, being absent, she replaced him with my friend, who happened to be at hand.

Madame de Montespan
Who was he?

Griffard
The one who held the candle.

Madame de Montespan
Oh!

(Mademoiselle Desoeillets restrains her.)

Griffard (pretending not to notice)
Yes, evidently this was an abuse of confidence, but after all, one witness is as good as another.

Madame de Montespan
La Voisin is a cheat, and your friend—

Griffard
Ah! Madame, he didn't expect to see what he saw and of which I dare not tell you the details. Once there, there was no way to get out of it. Besides, he was fascinated—fascinated, that's the word.

Madame de Montespan
In any case, he is unaware who is the heroine of this adventure?

Griffard
He has not named her.

Madame de Montespan
How would he know her name? She was masked, I suppose?

Griffard (confirming)
Yes, masked.

Madame de Montespan
Then, he doesn't know who she is?

Griffard
Yes, he says he can recognize her.

Madame de Montespan
By what signs?

Griffard
The figure, the pretty blonde hair.

Madame de Montespan
Around here, there's nothing but blonde hair.

Griffard
And then, the voice—haughty, imperious.

Madame de Montespan
Hardly enough. Is that all?

Griffard
One more thing. My friend was having trouble with that black candle and some wax spilled on the lady's shoulder. Right here.

(Griffard indicates her shoulder where she has a burn mark which she has hidden while pretending to play with her fan.)

Madame de Montespan
Still, that won't betray her, at least not if your friend has nothing more against her.

Griffard
Against her? Madame—what are you saying? He has no intention of noising this affair. He's much too gallant a man.

Madame de Montespan
And what does your friend want as the price of his discretion?

Griffard
Nothing for himself.

Madame de Montespan
Nothing—neither money, nor employment?

Griffard
Nothing.

Madame de Montespan
Then, I don't understand.

Griffard
He hopes that the great lady involved will, from pity of that unfortunate girl who is wrongly suspected of poisoning Mademoiselle de Fontanges—

Madame de Montespan
Suspected wrongly?

Griffard
Wrongly! That the great lady will employ her royal influence to save the child.

Madame de Montespan
And if she does?

Griffard
My friend will never disclose who the lady of last night was.

Madame de Montespan
And what happens if she doesn't?

Griffard
He will tell all.

Madame de Montespan
To—La Reynie?

Griffard
To the King.

Madame de Montespan
Without supporting proof?

Griffard
He will have some.

Madame de Montespan
The burn mark, right? And the imbecile thinks they will believe him?

Griffard
That's what he imagines, the imbecile.

Madame de Montespan (rising, menacing)
Tell your friend that if he doesn't want to be burned himself as an accomplice of Voisin, he'd better keep quiet. He can expect that!

Griffard
But he won't wait for it!

Madame de Montespan
We will see. Good day, Abbé.

Griffard
Oh, Madame won't ever be so charming as last night.

(Griffard bows, then goes to the buffet where he gets a drink.)

Madame de Montespan
The wretch. He needs a room in the Bastille.

Mademoiselle Desoeillets
I have a better idea.

(Madame de Montespan move to another group.)

Mademoiselle Desoeillets (to a lackey)
Fabien, you are going to follow this Abbé when he leaves and beat him. Leave him for dead. It's Madame's order and whatever happens you have nothing to fear. Understand? Go!

Madame de Montespan (to her entourage)
Good day, gentlemen. Come, Desoeillets.

(Madame de Montespan and Mademoiselle Desoeillets leave by the left. The other courtiers retire to the right. Griffard, who has observed Mademoiselle Desoeillets, starts to leave but is blocked by the master of the hotel.)

Master of the Hotel
Pardon, Monsieur. Where are you going?

Griffard
I am leaving.

Master of the Hotel
That way, monsieur. This side is the palace. (walking away)

Griffard
That way?

Valet
Yes. You follow the arbor to the Gate of the Dragon.

Griffard
Rather dark and lonely that way. (to master of the hotel, who is walking back) Tell me, my friend, is there no other way to leave than that?

Master of the Hotel
None at all, monsieur. Hurry, they are going to close the gate. (to one of the valets) What's wrong with him? He doesn't want to leave.

(Griffard goes to the left, stops, turns, comes back. He then goes to a table and takes two knives which he places in his pocket. Now, having been seen by the master of the hotel, he starts to leave again.)

Master of the Hotel (barring his way)
Ah, Abbé, Abbé.

Griffard
Excuse me?

All (surrounding him and singing)
Monsieur Abbé, Where are you running to?

Griffard
Gentlemen, gentlemen, I beg you.

Master of the Hotel
Permit me.

(The master of the hotel removes the knives from Griffard's pocket.)

Griffard
Oh, my God! Gentlemen, is it possible?

(A patrol of four guards comes up after a motion from the master of the hotel.)

Sergeant
Is this the one?

All
Yes.

Griffard (pretending to be astounded)
Oh, heavens! Are you arresting me?

All
It astounds him?

Sergeant
Come on, Monsieur Abbé, if you please.

Griffard
Monsieur—grace—pity!

Sergeant
Take your places. March.

Griffard (aside, relieved)
Ah, now I'm quite relieved.

(Griffard exits under guard.)

CURTAIN

ACT IV

La Reynie's Office

An usher is arranging papers on the table. La Reynie enters by the door at the right which the second usher opens for him.

La Reynie
Desgrez is here?

Usher
Yes, monsieur. In Monsieur Sagot's office.

La Reynie
Call him.

(La Reynie studies the papers on his desk while waiting. The usher goes to Sagot's office to get Desgrez, who then arrives.)

La Reynie
Has The Abbé Griffard been here in my absence?

Desgrez
No, monsieur.

La Reynie
Send to his rooms.

Desgrez
Useless, monsieur. I received a letter from him which hardly surprised me. He's in prison at Versailles for theft. I took it on myself to send two of my men to get him.

La Reynie
Advise me when he arrives.

(Desgrez goes back to Sagot's office. The main door opens and Colbert and Louvois enter.)

La Reynie
I've just come from St. Germain, gentlemen, where the King informed me that I was to have the honor of your visit.

Louvois
His Majesty, monsieur, at the express desire of Mademoiselle de Fontanges, who was unable to believe in the guilt of her lady of honor, commanded Monsieur Colbert and myself to assist in her interrogation before any arrest is made.

La Reynie
Since my arrival I gave the order to have her brought here.

Colbert
Monsieur d'Aquin assures us that Mademoiselle de Fontanges is out of danger.

Louvois
The attempt was made, none the less.

La Reynie
Assuredly.

Colbert
The Chamber Ardent will look into this doubtful case. How much does the King know?

La Reynie
Everything. His Majesty wishes to take part in the interrogations himself.

Usher (at the door)
The Chevalier de Tralage.

La Reynie
You can bring him in.

(Hector enters and bows to Louvois and Colbert.)

La Reynie
My nephew, Chevalier de Tralage.

Louvois
I've had the pleasure many times at Madame de Mainte-

non's.

Colbert
Who praises him much.

La Reynie
My nephew is here as a witness, if needed .Sit down, Hector.

First Usher
Monsieur Sagot is returned.

La Reynie
Let him come in.

(Sagot enters with dossiers. The usher closes the door.)

La Reynie
Monsieur Sagot, Clerk of the Chamber Ardent. These are the interrogatories?

Sagot
Yes, monsieur.

Louvois
La Voisin has confessed?

Sagot
No, monsieur, and her attitude is very different from those of the other accused. She affects the greatest tranquility, she sings, she laughs, she drinks! We found a letter on her

saying: "Keep quiet—we will save you."

(Colbert and Louvois rise and talk together at the right of the table. Hector also rises.)

Sagot (low to La Reynie)
Monsieur, I draw your attention to these passages marked in red ink. Monsieur de Bezons desires to confer with you before you see His Majesty.

La Reynie
Fine! I will see to this in a moment. Sit down, Monsieur Sagot. You come right in the nick of time to take some notes.

(Sagot sits and gets ready to write.)

Desgrez (coming from the right)
Mademoiselle D'Ormoize is here, monsieur.

La Reynie
Wait! (to Hector) I know from an indiscretion of Monsieur de Cessac, who met you Saturday at La Voisin's that you saw Mademoiselle D'Ormoize leaving there. Why didn't you tell me that?

Hector
De Cessac, monsieur, is very talkative. I didn't say I had recognized her, merely that I thought it looked like Mademoiselle D'Ormoize.

La Reynie
Meaning, Hector, that from generosity you didn't wish to reveal this clandestine visit which creates a very grave charge against her?

Hector
My God, monsieur!

La Reynie
From your discretion, one may conclude you fear the truth may harm her. (Hector makes a gesture) That's enough! (to Desgrez) Bring in Mademoiselle D'Ormoize.

(Colbert and Louvois sit to the right, La Reynie at the table, Hector on a chair. Desgrez brings in Solange.)

La Reynie
Sit down, mademoiselle. (Solange sits on a chair provided by Desgrez.) I don't have to remind you of the crime of which you are accused?

Solange
Very unjustly, monsieur, I assure you.

La Reynie
We hope so. You went Saturday, in the afternoon, to the home of this woman La Voisin. Monsieur de Tralage saw you there.

Solange
Yes, monsieur.

Louvois
And, why this hurry to escape from his view?

Solange
I was going for him, monsieur, but he was unaware of it.

La Reynie
Once again, the purpose of this visit?

Solange
I was very sad, monsieur, very discouraged. I went to consult this woman, like so many others, to know if I could hope to regain a lost happiness.

La Reynie
Meaning the love of this gentleman?

Solange
Yes, monsieur.

La Reynie
Taken by another woman?

Solange
Yes, monsieur.

La Reynie
For whom you naturally have feelings of jealousy and hate?

Solange
Oh, of jealousy, monsieur, yes. It's quite natural, but not of hate.

La Reynie
Still, you told Mademoiselle de Coetlegon yesterday morning: "Oh, soon she won't make me suffer any more."

Solange
Yes, monsieur, for after my visit to La Voisin, I counted on soon leaving Mademoiselle de Fontanges' service.

La Reynie
Still, you asked this woman for some elixir or powder.

Solange
Oh, no, monsieur, no. She is the one who proposed a philter to me—to make her drink. But I refused it, fearing it would make her ill.

La Reynie
If it wasn't to receive this philter, why did you return to La Voisin the same evening toward eight o'clock?

Solange
Me, monsieur?

La Reynie
Yes!

Solange
But I did not return to her, monsieur.

La Reynie
Are you very sure of that? You didn't return to Saint Germain?

Solange
No, monsieur

La Reynie
Where were you?

Solange
I went to the Church of Saint Roche for blessing.

La Reynie
Were you seen by someone who can testify to it?

Solange
Not that I know, monsieur.

(La Reynie exchanges looks with Louvois and Colbert.)

La Reynie
Then, you have no proof to support that statement. Are you sure you are not confusing the blessing at Saint Roche with a ceremony at La Voisin's—the Black Mass?

Solange
Oh!

La Reynie
You know what it is?

Solange
I have heard it spoken of, monsieur, as a horrible thing—in honor of the devil. That's all I know.

La Reynie
Well, we have reason to believe you assisted at this diabolic mass.

Solange
Me? What horror!

La Reynie
To prepare the poison poured by you the next day into the cup of milk.

Solange
But that's false, monsieur. That's false. And it's absurd. I am constantly at my service with Mademoiselle de Fontanges, who is ill. I am always giving her potions from Monsieur d'Aquin. It would be very easy for me to administer some bad beverage when I am alone with her—and no one would know it. I would be very stupid to do it in front of everyone.

Louvois
You might not have expected such a prompt effect.

Colbert
And milk taken from the buffet would be less suspect than a potion from a sick person's bedside.

Solange
Ah, God, with such arguments, who would not be guilty?

La Reynie
In short, you deny returning that evening to La Voisin's?

Solange
Yes—I deny it! Yes, yes, yes, I deny it!

La Reynie
Bring in the person who was there.

(Desgrez opens the door in the rear and brings in Mademoiselle Desoeillets.)

La Reynie
Marie Desoeillets, lady serving Madame de Montespan, do you wish, mademoiselle, to tell these gentlemen what you told me concerning Mademoiselle D'Ormoize.

Mademoiselle Desoeillets
Saturday evening, gentlemen, Madame de Montespan having given me several commission in Paris, I was coming back by way of the Rue Poissonnière in a carriage towards nine in the evening, when I saw Mademoiselle leave the Rue Beauregard.

Solange
Me?

Mademoiselle Desoeillets (without looking at her)
Oh, I recognized her very clearly. She wasn't masked and it was still light.

Solange
You saw me—me? You saw me at that time?

Mademoiselle Desoeillets
I thought it was some love intrigue and from discretion I went my way without seeming to see her.

Solange
But it wasn't me!

La Reynie (to Mademoiselle Desoeillets)
Are you indeed sure?

Mademoiselle Desoeillets
Oh, monsieur! I saw her just as I see you.

Solange (rising)
But this is false! This is false! Oh, evil woman, you are killing me with your lies.

La Reynie
You swear to it?

Mademoiselle Desoeillets
I swear it was Mademoiselle!

Solange
And I, I swear she is lying.

Mademoiselle Desoeillets
I swear that I speak the truth.

Solange
She's lying! She's lying! Oh, wretch, you are ruining me. What wrong have I done you?

Mademoiselle Desoeillets
And what reason would I have to lie?

La Reynie (to Solange)
Come on, confess.

Louvois
Admit the truth.

Colbert
To deserve some pity.

Solange
I don't want pity! I want justice.

Louvois
Don't oblige us to force the truth out of you.

Solange
Oh, if you hurt me, I will confess anything you wish. That doesn't prevent me from being innocent.

La Reynie
That's all! (to Desgrez) Conduct Mademoiselle to the Bastille.

(Desgrez steps toward her.)

Solange (rising excitedly)
No, no, I don't wish it! Leave me alone! Leave me alone! (she repulses Desgrez) Gentlemen! Gentlemen! I am innocent. I swear it on the salvation of my soul. Before God who hears me and will punish her.

La Reynie
Desgrez.

Solange
No! No! (she runs to Hector) Monsieur, from pity, defend me. Don't let me be taken away by that man. You know I am not a woman who would kill someone—you, you know it. Tell them then, that I am not capable. Tell them. Tell them.

(Hector is overwhelmed. He dries her eyes without looking at her.)

Solange
Oh, you believe it, too. You! (to Desgrez) Oh God, take

me away from him—take me away from him, and do with me whatever you wish.

(Desgrez leads her off to the right.)

La Reynie
You can leave, Hector. But this is partly your fault.

Hector (very moved)
Ah, monsieur. I'll never forgive myself for it in this life.

(Hector leaves by the left. The door is closed after him.)

Le Reynie (to Louvois and Colbert)
Well, gentlemen, you are convinced, as I am. (to Mademoiselle Desoeillets) I don't need to keep you any longer, Mademoiselle.

(Mademoiselle Desoeillets curtsies and goes to the door. Upon opening it she is confronted by Griffard, who bars her way. She retreats before him. He takes a step forward and Mademoiselle Desoeillets thinks to get by him but he blocks her again, without seeming to.)

La Reynie
It's our Abbé! Come in, come in, Monsieur Griffard. We are finished. What is this business of theft?

Griffard (pointing to Mademoiselle Desoeillets)
No one, monsieur, can better inform you than this lady.

Mademoiselle Desoeillets (very troubled)
Me?

La Reynie (startled)
Mademoiselle Desoeillets?

Griffard
She will explain that after I had a conversation with a certain lady, I thought it wise to be under the protection of the police.

La Reynie (to Mademoiselle Desoeillets)
You hear?

Mademoiselle Desoeillets
Monsieur! Monsieur! Don't believe a word this man says.

Griffard (tranquilly)
Me, I will say nothing. I am going to let you do all the talking.

La Reynie
Now, what is there between you and him?

Mademoiselle Desoeillets (exasperated by Griffard's smiling face and losing her composure)
There—oh, this Abbé. He's a scoundrel, monsieur, a rogue who has sworn to betray us.

La Reynie
Us?

Griffard
Go on, my dear. A good start. Continue. Speak!

Mademoiselle Desoeillets (between her teeth)
Oh! Demon!

Griffard
To betray us? By whom? Answer. Us—who is us?

Mademoiselle Desoeillets
Me—and—

La Reynie
Who?

Mademoiselle Desoeillets
Madame!

(Exclamations by Colbert and La Reynie.)

Louvois
Your mistress?

Mademoiselle Desoeillets
He threatened to denounce her about this affair.

La Reynie
Of the poisons! To denounce—

Louvois and Colbert
The Marquise!

Griffard (tranquilly)
You've done it! Thank you, my dear, you spared me the trouble.

Louvois
But this is absurd!

Colbert
This man is crazy!

Mademoiselle Desoeillets
Oh! He's not crazy! But—

(Sagot opens his dossier and shows a passage to La Reynie.)

La Reynie
Pardon! Gentlemen, I beg you— (to Desgrez) Desgrez, take Mademoiselle.

Desgrez
Free?

La Reynie
Secretly and under careful guard.

(Colbert and Louvois are stupefied.)

Mademoiselle Desoeillets
Me!

La Reynie (to Desgrez)
Quickly! Quickly!

Mademoiselle Desoeillets (as she is led off by Desgrez to the right)
Oh, this man, this man! (to Griffard) Oh, wretch, you will pay dearly for this.

Louvois (to La Reynie)
What do you mean, monsieur?

La Reynie
Listen to this passage from the interrogation of Voisin's daughter which was just brought to my attention. The girl tried to strangle herself in prison. Question: Where were you the morning your mother was arrested? Reply: I was going to Saint Germain to deliver the powders prepared after the Black Mass.

Griffard
Oh!

La Reynie
Question: To deliver them to whom? Reply: To Mademoiselle Desoeillets. Question: What were these powders? Reply Love powders to preserve to Madame de Montespan the love of the King.

(He puts the dossier on the table for Colbert and Louvois to read.)

Colbert
Well, the girl can say what she wants.

Louvois
Doubtless.

(Sagot puts another paper before La Reynie, which he glances at, then starts to read.)

Louvois
The interrogation of The Abbé Guibourg. He confesses to saying the Black Mass for Madame de Montespan who was masked. He also says he's done it several times for her over the years.

Colbert
And how does he know the masked woman was Madame de Montespan?

Louvois?
Yes?

La Reynie
He was asked that. Here is his reply: "At one of the first masses, under the chalice was written on a parchment 'I ask that the King continue to love me, that my children be recognized as princes, and that the Queen be repudiated so I can marry the King.'" Only Madame de Montespan could have asked that. Moreover, the servant Margot, Lesage, and Marguerite confirm the same dates and the same details.

Louvois
And, if all these rascals were making this up in the hope we wouldn't dare try them, just by embarrassing Madame de Montespan?

Colbert
Or simply to gain some time?

La Reynie
The accused, from the time of arrest, were all isolated and questioned separately. No cooperation is possible.

Colbert
At present. But, they might have concocted it in advance.

La Reynie
So be it! But The Abbé Griffard is not party to their plot.

Louvois
Do you formally accuse her?

Griffard
Oh, yes, I accuse her.

Colbert
You recognized her as the masked woman?

Griffard
Absolutely.

Louvois
And you told her this?

Griffard
Explicitly.

Colbert
And she admitted it?

Griffard
No! She denied it.

Louvois and Colbert
Ah!

Griffard
But, without knowing it, she gave herself away! Then she threatened to kill me if I mentioned her name.

Colbert
On a simple suspicion?

Louvois
Without proofs to support it?

Griffard
Without proofs? I have one—and a very damning one.

Colbert and Louvois
Which is?

Griffard
Allow me to hold it in reserve—in the likelihood I may have to defend myself.

Colbert
You foresee that?

Griffard
Oh, monsieur, when a poor devil like me attacks such a powerful person, he can expect anything. I am expecting it and I am prepared!

Louvois (moving his chair)
Gentlemen, we have to talk. Let Monsieur Griffard and Sagot leave us for a little while.

La Reynie
Monsieur Griffard, will you wait with Monsieur Sagot?

Griffard (bowing)
Whatever you like, monsieur.

(Sagot and Griffard go into Sagot's office.)

Louvois
You are very polite, monsieur, to this gazetteer.

La Reynie
He has just rendered us a signal service.

Louvois
Which may do a lot of harm if we don't put things in good order. These sad revelations are a serious test of our zeal for His Majesty. What is your opinion on the guilt of Madame de Montespan?

Colbert
Unfortunately, very likely.

La Reynie
And for me, very certain.

Louvois
It is a point I am sure on which we are all agreed. And also that the Marquise can never be brought to trial. No one must know of this.

Colbert
Assuredly. Her name cannot be mentioned.

La Reynie
We cannot lose sight of the fact that the King is aware of all I knew or thought I knew of this unfortunate affair. He is anxiously awaiting the result of the first interrogations. What shall we do?

Louvois
The simplest and in reality the only thing to do. Blame it all on Mademoiselle D'Ormoize, but with the help of Mademoiselle de Fontanges obtain the King's forgiveness for her.

La Reynie
Declared guilty?

Louvois
Without hesitation!

La Reynie (hesitating)
It's a measure—

Louvois
Harsh! I agree. But can you think of a better?

La Reynie
I would prefer one which put both Madame de Montespan and Mademoiselle D'Ormoize out of danger.

Louvois
That's impossible! If we declare Mademoiselle D'Ormoize not guilty, then the King will naturally ask who is guilty. He won't allow the crime to go unpunished.

La Reynie
But the Chamber Ardent—

Louvois
The Chamber Ardent is not the Parliament. It understands its duties as we do. The thing to do is suppress the interrogations. Declare to the accusers that we see only slanders in their statements against Madame de Montespan—an attempt to hide behind her. Shorten the procedure. Expedite the execution of La Voisin, her daughter, Guibourg,

Lesage! Release Mademoiselle D'Ormoize instantly. And for the rest, deport them to Canada or Santo Domingo.

Louvois
In a month the affair will be over. And Madame de Montespan will be saved. There won't be a single witness, a single proof, a single accuser.

La Reynie
Pardon, monsieur, there is still one.

Louvois
The Abbé.

La Reynie
Whom the King wishes to interrogate.

Louvois
He won't give us any trouble. He's much too smart not to bend to our will. Call him—and we will teach him his role.

La Reynie (calling)
Monsieur Griffard! Come, I beg you!

(Griffard enters.)

Louvois
Take a seat! Take a seat, I beg you. We are all agreed to suppress this interrogation and to leave His Majesty in ignorance of the role played in this scandal by Madame de Montespan. It's necessary that you be informed.

Griffard
Me, monsieur?

Louvois
Yes! You will have the honor of being questioned by the King. Your declaration must agree with ours.

Griffard
I am not a judge, monsieur, and for my part, I see no reason not to leave Madame de Montespan in the shadow.

Colbert (approvingly)
That's it.

Louvois
Very good.

Griffard
But in this situation, what will become of Mademoiselle D'Ormoize?

Louvois
We are considering.

Griffard
She won't be set free?

Louvois
Impossible. To release Mademoiselle D'Ormoize is to implicate the Marquise.

Colbert
You don't have to identify the unknown—with Mademoiselle D'Ormoize—but simply to tell His Majesty that you don't know who she is. (pause) The rest is our concern.

Griffard
I don't wish harm to anyone, but this young girl?

Colbert
This scruple is praiseworthy, but excessive. It is a question of superior interest.

Griffard
I know of no interest superior to justice and humanity.

Colbert
It's a case of adopting a measure which injures only one person but profits all the others.

Griffard
Gentlemen, I am not a religious man, but this—

Louvois
Don't you allow for an individual to be sacrificed for the community?

Griffard
If it's voluntary—certainly. That's heroism. If it is imposed, it is nothing but martyrdom.

Colbert
Martyrdom—so be it! It is beautiful to suffer for one's King.

Griffard
We must get Mademoiselle D'Ormoize's opinion.

(Louvois makes a gesture of impatience, but is calmed by Colbert.)

Colbert
It's a case of accepting a small evil for a great benefit. Public morality would be outraged if this became known.

Griffard
I agree to that. But the only way to avoid it is to take the position that the King does justice no matter how closely it touches his own person or his closest associates.

Colbert
You are mad!

Louvois
We must suffocate this affair at any price.

Griffard
I would like to do so; but not at the price of Mademoiselle D'Ormoize.

Colbert
You can't place this girl in balance with the shame to the

state, to the King, that the affair must insure.

Griffard
I can't conceive of any greater taint on royal prestige than this shameful condemnation of Mademoiselle D'Ormoize.

Colbert
But there's no shame. It will be a secret.

Louvois
It will seem to be a merit.

Griffard
But that's exactly what I find to be revolting.

Louvois (upset)
Bourgeois morality has nothing to do with this! It cannot regulate the duty of a Minister.

Griffard
Then, monsieur, he must suffer for it, when his duty is not that of an honest man.

(Louvois makes a gesture of rage. He is restrained by Le Reynie.)

Louvois
Monsieur, you are strangely abusing the patience we are expending in convincing you.

Griffard
We are philosophizing, monsieur. I will bow to your arguments if I find them convincing.

Colbert (ingratiatingly)
Let's see, let's see, Abbé. Let's think it through. Government is not possible without discreet measures to which all laws must bend—The Reason of State.

Griffard
That's a reason given in place of others. When someone vanishes, the question is: Was it down by a criminal or a Minister?

(Louvois is furious.)

Colbert
Perhaps it's the memory of your own wrongs that makes you so reluctant?

Griffard
Not at all. I just wish to protect Mademoiselle D'Ormoize—nothing more.

Colbert
Well, she'll be all right!

(Louvois stares at Colbert, but Colbert gestures to him.)

Colbert
Did we say we were going to send her to the execution?

Not at all. We will inter her in some provincial convent where she will be well cared for and, after a while, we'll find an honest marriage for her and a good dowry. Look—what the devil—you are not her brother, her father, or her lover, are you?

Griffard
Me? I only saw her for the first time in my life yesterday—and have never spoken to her.

Colbert
Then, why do you espouse her cause so hotly?

Griffard
Because she had only me to defend her.

Louvois
Do you persist in your refusal?

Griffard
Yes, monsieur, I persist.

Louvois (breaking away from Colbert who is trying to restrain him)
That's enough! No more discussion. I forbid you to tell His Majesty a single word which can endanger Madame de Montespan.

Griffard
I must consult my conscience.

Louvois (violently)
I have nothing to do with your conscience. I order you to obey, that's all.

Griffard
I don't have the same reasons you do to sacrifice this young woman. And I won't aid something I consider to be a crime.

Colbert
You say what!

Griffard
A crime! You have no right to withhold this information—the truth—from His Majesty.

Louvois
You will tell the King?

Griffard
Everything. Including your attempt to silence me.

Louvois
You will tell him nothing.

Griffard
I differ—

Louvois
Nothing! You are not going to see him.

Griffard
Monsieur!

La Reynie (protesting)
The King has commanded me.

Louvois (beside himself)
Well, I forbid it.

La Reynie
But—

Louvois
I forbid it! And I take it on myself. The King will understand why I spared him the sight of a factious rebel, a mad man—

Griffard
Me?

Louvois
Escaped from the galley.

Griffard
Take care, monsieur.

Louvois
You dare?

Griffard
Take care of preventing me from seeing the King.

Louvois (almost crazy)
Threats! To me!

Griffard
The King—

Louvois (no longer listening)
This is too much insolence.

Colbert (trying to calm him)
Monsieur—

Louvois (to La Reynie)
Put this comedian in the Bastille.

Griffard
I tell you, I will defend myself.

Louvois
He's still railing! In a cell—in the basement—

Griffard
Reason of State.

Louvois
And if he's still insolent, the whip!

Griffard
Why not death?

Louvois
We will see later if it would be better to return him to the galleys and let him rot there.

Griffard
An execution.

Louvois (to La Reynie)
You heard me, monsieur. (La Reynie bows) Come, monsieur, come. We have nothing more to do here.

(Louvois and Colbert leave. The usher closes the door after them.)

Griffard
Monsieur! Monsieur! You promised me that whatever might happen, I would be free.

La Reynie
Yes, but—

Griffard
You swore it, monsieur. And they are arresting me. For telling the truth.

La Reynie
It's an order of the Minister. I must obey.

Griffard
And you are going to do what?

La Reynie
Obey him! I arrest you.

Griffard
Oh.

La Reynie
But all prisoners have the right to escape. (pointing to the door) Escape by the side entrance and good luck.

Griffard
Ah, monsieur. I am sure of it.

La Reynie
Where are you going to go?

Griffard
To the King.

La Reynie
You are risking your head.

Griffard
I will risk it. The cause is worth it. Till we meet again, monsieur.

La Reynie
Abbé! (Griffard turns in the doorway) You are a brave man.

Griffard
Well, monsieur, that goes for both of us.

(Griffard disappears.)

CURTAIN

ACT V

The King's Palace at St. Germain

The King's room—bedchamber. Window opening on a balcony. The room is lit by candelabra. Ladies and courtiers are seated and standing, talking.

Madame d'Humières
They interrogated the accused this morning. Several important people are badly compromised—but no one knows who for sure.

Madame de Brissac
And the King is very preoccupied with it.

De Brionne
Lower! His Majesty is on the balcony.

Madame d'Humières
Much too far to hear us.

De Dommeyrac
What is certain is that at three this morning, the Countess

de Soissons and the Marquise d'Allunye left quietly by carriage.

Madame de Nevers
The couldn't betray themselves more clumsily.

Madame de Brissac
Yes. Her conscience is blacker than her complexion, la Mancini.

De Brionne
The death of the Count of Soissons has been suspected for a long time.

De Dommeyrac
And the attempted assassination of Mademoiselle de la Vallière.

(The ladies exclaim.)

Madame de Nevers (to Madame d'Humières)
Come now!

Madame de Brissac
Assassination?

Madame d'Humières
Is it possible?

De Dommeyrac
It's an old story and kept quiet. But I already know the

best part. Madame de Soissons was enraged to be supplanted by Mademoiselle de la Vallière, so she introduced two ragamuffins into La Vallière's quarters with orders to strangle her in her sleep. They were opening the window when La Vallière was awakened by the noise and put them to flight.

(The King leaves the balcony and comes forward with Colbert.)

De Brionne
The King.

(All rise respectfully.)

King
So, monsieur, Mademoiselle D'Ormoize doesn't admit it?

Colbert
Far from it, Sire. Louvois and La Reynie will tell you as I do.

King
D'Aquin says Mademoiselle de Fontanges was not poisoned. But Mademoiselle D'Ormoize will always be guilty of having assisted at this sacrilegious mass. I will talk it over shortly with Monsieur de La Reynie, who is here—and tomorrow with Monsieur de Louvois.

(La Reynie enters through a door at the left which is opened by an usher. He carries a large portfolio of red Moroccan leather.)

King
Good evening, monsieur.

(Colbert bows.)

King (to the company)
Ladies, when you have taken leave of the Queen, I suggest you go down to the buffet. It's delicious by moonlight.

Madame d'Humières.
Your Majesty won't add his presence to this delicious nocturnal affair?

King
No, regretfully. I have to work this evening with Monsieur de La Reynie. Ladies, I won't keep you any longer.

(The King bows to them and the ladies curtsey, then leave.)

King
You are alone, monsieur? I told you to bring that man—what's his name?

La Reynie
The Abbé Griffard, Sire. But Monsieur de Louvois, after having spoken with him, thought he was not a person to whom Your Majesty could give an audience, and ordered me to lodge him in the Bastille.

King
Mr. Colbert told me nothing of this.

La Reynie
An oversight.

King
Monsieur de Louvois permits himself to contradict my orders too often. He will end by irritating me. Send for The Abbé.

La Reynie
Unfortunately, Sire, before being arrested, he escaped. The man has a positive genius for escape.

King
Try to find him.

La Reynie
We are already working on that very enthusiastically. In place of The Abbé I have brought the preliminary interrogations you wished to see. (handing dossiers to the King) They compromised certain persons so much that I have proceeded to make immediate arrests. For those persons of greater importance, Your Majesty, in consideration of their quality, must decide what to do with them.

King
Is there much to this case?

La Reynie
Alas, yes, Sire. Those whom we would hardly suspect are involved.

King
Sit down and let's see.

(La Reynie sits.)

La Reynie
The number of women involved in this case is quite considerable.

King
Their weapon is poison.

La Reynie
The most compromised are as follows— (noise at door) Excuse me, Sire, someone is knocking at the door.

King
See!

(La Reynie goes to the door and opens it.)

La Reynie
Monsieur de Tralage, my nephew.

King
Let him enter.

(Hector enters and La Reynie closes the door.)

Hector
I bring this letter to His Majesty from Madame de Maintenon who requests a reply.

King
Give it here. (reading) This is amazing! The Abbé is under Madame de Maintenon's protection and wishes to see me. (to Hector) Bring him here right away.

(Hector goes out.)

La Reynie
The Abbé is a remarkable man. We are about to touch on certain matters that are so unpleasant that Monsieur de Louvois was of the opinion that Your Majesty should be spared.

King
Monsieur de Louvois is too zealous. I allow for no infractions of my orders. I told him, and it astonishes me to have to repeat it. I want the truth—the whole truth.

La Reynie
The Countess of Soissons, who fled this morning, before I could do anything—

King
Advised by me to get out of France. I thought she must be guilty. It is a weakness for which I may have to answer to

God.

La Reynie
The Duchess de Bouillon and—

King
Go on.

La Reynie
The Marquise de Montespan.

King
Are you losing your mind?

(La Reynie pushes an interrogation to the King. The King reads slowly, then lets out an exclamation.)

King (shaking)
It isn't possible. These are odious lies.

La Reynie (tensely)
Sire!

(The King regains his control.)

La Reynie
We thought at first that all these swine were slandering her in order to hide behind her.

King
Indeed, it's very possible.

La Reynie
Unfortunately, Sire, that idea did not withstand examination.

King
Ring for an usher.

La Reynie (ringing)
Yes, Sire.

(An usher appears immediately.)

King
Madame de Montespan is at her service with the Queen. I wish to speak to her at once.

(The usher bows and glides out as noiselessly as he came.)

La Reynie
There is, moreover, a witness who confirmed these interrogations without knowing of them and who is not a suspect.

King
Let him come! Let him come!

La Reynie (seeing the door at the right open)
He's here.

(Hector comes in with Griffard, then waits for orders.)

King
Chevalier, wait for my orders in that room, please.

(The King points to a door at the left. Hector bows and goes out.)

King (to Griffard)
Come here, monsieur. (Griffard advances and bows) You are absolutely sure of what Monsieur de La Reynie has just told me. (watching him carefully)

Griffard
Had I the least doubt I would not dare to appear before Your Majesty.

King
Take care not to make so grave an accusation without convincing proofs.

Griffard
I believe I have one which is irrefutable.

King
Tell me.

Griffard
It will have more force if given by Madame de Montespan herself.

(An usher comes in and whispers to La Reynie.)

La Reynie
Madame de Montespan is here.

King (to Griffard)
Go there in the alcove by the window. Wait until I call you.

(Griffard effectively disappears into the shadows. The King signals the usher to bring in La Montespan.)

Madame de Montespan (entering, smiling)
Your Majesty has called me?

King
Yes, Madame—about this affair of—poisoning.

Madame de Montespan
But, I thought Mademoiselle de Fontanges was just sick. That's what d'Aquin said. Madame d'Humières didn't poison her, nor did anyone else.

King
True. But there's more to it. Look at these interrogatories, please.

Madame de Montespan
Huh? (she looks)

King
Yes.

(Madame de Montespan reads, then breaks out in a loud laugh.)

Madame de Montespan
Oh! Oh! What silliness! (pointing to La Reynie) Is this the gentleman who brought you this nonsense?

King (disgusted)
You find it funny?

Madame de Montespan
You don't think I am going to take it tragically? (pushes the papers away) I have already had a visit from a certain Abbé, their accomplice, who wanted me to purchase his silence.

King
The Abbé Griffard perhaps?

Madame de Montespan
Perhaps. I don't have the honor of remembering his name.

King
And, what did this Abbé say?

Madame de Montespan (gaily)
Oh, some insanities. He said something about denouncing me to Monsieur de La Reynie. Didn't he tell you he saw me at this fortune teller's, where he supposedly saw me involved in I don't know what ceremony?

La Reynie
He told me that, in substance.

Madame de Montespan (bitterly)
And you let him say it?

La Reynie
My duty, Madame, is to listen.

Madame de Montespan (haughtily)
And as for me, Monsieur, I don't allow you to lend your ear to lies that dishonor me.

King
And I, Madame, do you allow me?

Madame de Montespan (turning to the King)
Your Majesty means?

King
I mean to know what's going on.

Madame de Montespan
You believe me capable—me? Me?

King
I will believe what is proper. If this priest lies, he will pay dearly, but if he speaks the truth—

(The King signals La Reynie to introduce Griffard.)

Madame de Montespan
The truth? These horrors?

King
We are going to find out. Come in, monsieur.

Madame de Montespan (turning)
Here? This man! Your Majesty imposes the sight of this wretch on me?

(Madame de Montespan falls into an armchair.)

King
You ought to be in a hurry, as I am, Madame, to confront him and prove your innocence.

Madame de Montespan
I refuse a test unworthy of me. This man is a bandit. That suffices. And I don't admit his word can be put in balance with mine.

King
And I, Madame, do not admit that anyone can accuse you falsely of such infamies without being punished.

Madame de Montespan
I won't lower myself to—

King
I beg you to be quiet.

Madame de Montespan
But, Sire.

(Madame de Montespan rises, but at a look from the King, falls back into her seat.)

Madame de Montespan
Oh!

King (to Griffard)
Nearer, monsieur, nearer. You swear that Madame was present at the ceremony the other night?

Griffard (simply)
I swear it.

Madame de Montespan
Oh! Before me! He has the impudence.

(A gesture of the King cuts off her words.)

King
You say you can prove what you say.

Griffard
As great a proof as your Majesty could wish.

Madame de Montespan (affecting to laugh)
Oh! Oh!

King
Give it.

Griffard
This morning, Sire, La Voisin's daughter brought to Mademoiselle Desoeillets certain powders to be given to Madame. (pointing to Madame de Montespan)

Madame de Montespan
That is false.

Griffard (tranquilly, pointing to the dossier)
The testimony of that girl is there.

(Madame de Montespan looks at the dossier, then at Griffard.)

Griffard
These powders were concocted the night after the mass—

Madame de Montespan (exasperated)
Eh! What has that to do with me?

King (cutting her off with a gesture)
Go on!

Griffard
The same as Madame has had recourse to in years past to assure herself of the love of Your Majesty.

Madame de Montespan (rising, trying to attack Griffard)
You lie, rogue. You lie!

(A gesture from the King stops her in her tracks.)

Griffard (tranquilly taking a step toward her)
But what Madame is unaware of is that the friends of Monsieur Fouquet, no longer hoping for the King's mercy, have conspired with La Voisin to kill His Majesty and unknown to you, Madame, these powders were poisoned.

King
Good God!

(Madame de Montespan is terrified. Griffard goes to the table and pours some lemonade into a goblet, and holds it in his hand.)

Griffard
La Voisin made a fool of you, Madame. She knew you would give these powders to the King, as you have in the past. Now, if all this is a lie, if La Voisin's daughter didn't bring these powders to you, if you were not the heroine of the other night and if, with the aid of your lackey, these powders were not placed by you in the King's lemonade—why then, everything I say is a lie, and the King may drink without fear. (offers the glass to the King) But, if I am telling the truth—why, he's a dead man.

King
You hear, Madame?

Madame de Montespan (wildly)
Yes, yes, I hear.

(The King takes the goblet from Griffard. Madame de Montespan leaps to stop him.)

Madame de Montespan
No—no—don't drink it, Louis!

(Then, realizing she's completely given herself away, she falls sobbing into a chair.)

King (to La Reynie and Griffard)
Go there. (pointing to a door) Gentlemen, I beg you. Don't go away and return when I call.

(La Reynie and Griffard bow and go toward the door.)

La Reynie
You win, my friend.

Griffard (low)
No. If the King weakens, my score is zero.

(Exit La Reynie and Griffard.)

King
So, it's true? What this man says? What is written here? It's true? You went to this poisoner's house? You lent yourself to these ignoble practices! You wanted me to drink this filthy drink? It's true? Answer me, you stupid

woman!

Madame de Montespan (in a low voice, tearfully)
But, it's all your fault. You are the one who forced me.

(The King stares at her.)

Madame de Montespan
It's you! And, if I am guilty, you are more guilty than I am! Because of your betrayals, you made me despair and condemned me to such means to protect myself.

King
I? I forced you? I?

Madame de Montespan (miserably)
Haven't you been cruel enough! Haven't you humiliated me before those rivals that you produce every time I turn around and to whom I must smile? How many have there been? Your Fontanges! Your Maintenon! It's to keep you from them that I have had recourse to that woman. It's frightful! It's horrible. But you can't force me into committing a crime and not pardon me for having committed it from love of you.

King
Pardon what is written here! Read it! Read it! Forget that! I will always have those infamies before my eyes. Oh, yes, yes—it's really finished. I no longer have anything but scorn and disgust for you.

Madame de Montespan
Go on—say it. You are very glad to find a pretext to be free of me.

King
You call this a pretext?

Madame de Montespan
It will do to get rid of me, right? Like that bawling baby La Vallière who only knew how to weep.

(Madame de Montespan stands up. She's angry.)

King
It doesn't become you to make fun of a woman I sacrificed to you. She really loved me. And in her distress, she didn't turn to the devil—she turned to God.

Madame de Montespan
To whom you consigned her willingly enough.

(This barb hits the King.)

Madame de Montespan
I suppose you want me to go to a cloister like her, right?

King
It would be better for your sins.

Madame de Montespan
And yours! (sitting down again) But don't count on it. I

am not resigned, not a penitent. I don't see myself as a nun.

(She turns her back to him.)

King
No. You're ambitions, egoistic and vain. And you never loved anything in me except the King.

Madame de Montespan (waving a hand)
Oh, Louis. You know that is not true. As for my pride—

King
Yes. Let's talk about that.

Madame de Montespan (swiftly)
Let's talk about yours instead. People must adore you like a god!

King
The god was human enough for you and provided you with a good life.

Madame de Montespan (without even looking at him)
A good life! Mine? A peasant woman can trust her man better than I can trust your royal word of honor! You are the most egotistical man alive. And all you ever say to any complaint is: "I don't want to be disturbed." (mimicking him)

King
Infected by your execrable perfumes.

Madame de Montespan
Don't slander my perfumes. You are very ungrateful. Madame de Maintenon will tell you just the same as I do.

King
There is nothing between her and me, as you think.

Madame de Montespan
You haven't done it yet? So she is still holding you off and dangling the sugar plum in your face? But the hour is coming when she will tell you—eyes raised to heaven—that she's decided to do it for your salvation.

King
The accomplice of La Voisin is welcome to outrage an honest woman.

Madame de Montespan
Oh, surely you won't call her a Bacchante as you did me. Oh, no! She is reason itself. No temperament, no heart. She loves with a pious love, totally confined to devotion and chaste transports authorized by the Church.

King
Shut up!

Madame de Montespan (arms crossed defiantly)
And then, the widow of Scarron will sugar your tea and

clean your bed. Old libertines always end up with chamber maids.

King (in a rage, going toward her)
Shut up! Shut up!

Madame de Montespan
And she's clever enough to convince you her husband left her hymen still intact. And her lover, too.

King (threatening)
This is too much.

Madame de Montespan (tranquilly)
Don't shout so loud. They'll think you are beating me!

King (calming down)
Tomorrow you will leave the court.

Madame de Montespan
Me?

King
And you will live in a retreat I will choose for you.

Madame de Montespan
Exile me—shut me up in some province—you are joking.

King (cold and resolved)
You will leave, I tell you—tomorrow.

Madame de Montespan
Not tomorrow, not ever!

King
I know how to make you.

Madame de Montespan
I defy you!

King
Oh!

(The King goes to ring.)

Madame de Montespan
I defy you to do it. You will kick me out like a servant—the mother of your children!

(The King stops, his hand on the bell.)

Madame de Montespan
You wouldn't dare create such a scandal. You will smother this affair. You will burn these papers.

King
No.

Madame de Montespan (continuing)
And I will stay at the palace with my rank, my title, my wealth. We are finished, you and I. But I will keep my crown. We've already had one Queen at this court. Now

there will be two—that's all. Go to your duenna and do penance with her for the pleasures you once had with me. And regret them!

King (ringing)
Remorse yes, regrets no. (to the usher who appears) Light the way for Madame.

Madame de Montespan
Good night.

(Madame de Montespan exits. The King rings again. Griffard, La Reynie and Hector return.)

King
Come in, gentlemen. (beckons to La Reynie to whom he speaks in a low voice) Does Mademoiselle D'Ormoize know who was really at that mass?

La Reynie
She is completely ignorant of it, as is my nephew.

King
Who offered to marry her, you told me?

La Reynie
Yes, Sire.

King
Let him come here. We have seen the light, Chevalier, Mademoiselle D'Ormoize is innocent.

Hector
Ah, Sire! How nice for her and for me. Pardon—I forget myself.

King
Not at all! Not at all! (writes an order) Your joy pleases me. This order is for her release. You may take it yourself if you like.

Hector
Will Your Majesty allow me to proceed at once?

King
Yes, go, go! (Hector bows and moves toward the door) But, I owe her reparation. I shall give her a large dowry. Tomorrow you will present her to Madame de Maintenon.

Hector
Oh, Sire, how many kindnesses.

(Hector leaves.)

King (to La Reynie)
That leaves only one witness—this priest—who is one too many.

La Reynie (uneasy)
Ah, Sire, he is your savior.

King (motioning to Griffard to come close)
Monsieur, you know too many things of which you ought

to be unaware.

Griffard (in the most natural tone)
Me, Sire? I know nothing.

King (surprised)
Huh?

Griffard
But, nothing at all. Absolutely nothing!

King
That's the way to talk, monsieur. Don't depart from that and we'll discuss the price of your ignorance.

Griffard
My liberty, Sire, is sufficient.

King
To your taste! Not mine.

Griffard
Well, since Your Majesty has the goodness to insist, a small, small office in the Royal Library would answer my wishes.

King
You shall have it. The best. And I don't consider myself quits with you. (to La Reynie as he starts to leave) Tomorrow morning, monsieur, to burn what is there. (pointing to the dossier) Good night, gentlemen.

(The King exits. Griffard and La Reynie look at each other. Griffard falls into a chair while La Reynie collects the papers.)

Griffard
Ouf!

CURTAIN

ABOUT FRANK J. MORLOCK

FRANK J. MORLOCK has written and translated many plays since retiring from the legal profession in 1992. His translations have also appeared on Project Gutenberg, the Alexandre Dumas Père web page, Literature in the Age of Napoléon, Infinite Artistries.com, and Munsey's (formerly Blackmask). In 2006 he received an award from the North American Jules Verne Society for his translations of Verne's plays. He lives and works in México.

www.ingramcontent.com/pod-product-compliance
Lightning Source LLC
LaVergne TN
LVHW041617070426
835507LV00008B/291